LEADING SCHOOLS II

C000132756

GOVERNANCE AND GOVERNORS

ESSAYS IN LEADERSHIP
FOR CHANGING TIMES

Edited by

Nigel Richardson and Stuart Westley

Published for the Association of Governing Bodies of Independent
Schools and the Headmasters' and Headmistresses' Conference
by John Catt Educational Ltd

2012

First Published 2012

by John Catt Educational Ltd,
12 Deben Mill Business Centre, Old Maltings Approach,
Melton, Woodbridge, Suffolk IP12 1BL
Tel: 01394 389850 Fax: 01394 386893
Email: enquiries@johncatt.com
Website: www.johncatt.com

Opinions expressed in this publication are those of the contributors and are not
necessarily those of the publishers or the sponsors. We cannot accept responsibility
for any errors or omissions.

ISBN: 978 1 908 095 299
eISBN: 978 1 908 095 435

Set and designed by
John Catt Educational Limited

Printed and bound in Great Britain
by The MANSON Group Limited

CONTENTS

About the Contributors

Chris Brown read English at Cambridge, undertook his teaching practice at Marlborough, and subsequently taught at The Leys and Pangbourne before moving to Radley. Having been Head of English and Director of Studies, he became Head of Norwich School (1984-2002). He chaired the HMC Inspection Steering Group; was a member of the original Independent Schools Inspectorate (ISI) Committee, and was a qualified reporting inspector for HMC and then for ISI. He was Chairman of HMC in 2001. He now acts as an educational consultant appraising Heads and senior staff, as well as helping governing bodies in the selection of Heads.

Alan Browne is an Associate Director with Arup (Ove Arup & Partners Limited), in the Programme and Project Management practice. An engineer by background, he has specialised in managing building projects and programmes for clients. He also advises clients on estates strategies, site acquisitions and mergers. He works in a range of market sectors including schools and universities and has been delivering building projects for over 30 years.

Matthew Burgess is General Secretary of the Independent Schools Council (ISC). After education at Brighton College and a law degree at Queens' College, Cambridge, he has 20 years experience as a solicitor. He leads ISC's work, on behalf of almost 1,300 independent schools, to protect and promote the sector with policy makers and opinion formers; to be a leading source of legal and regulatory guidance for the sector; and to conduct and compile authoritative sector research and intelligence. Previously he worked for Centrica advising the FTSE100 group on strategically significant transactions; with Linklaters in Singapore and London; and Gouldens in London. He is a Fulbright Fellow and a governor of two ISC schools.

Jonathan Cook was General Secretary of the Independent Schools' Bursars' Association (ISBA) from 2005-2010. Prior to this, he was a soldier for 34 years and then Bursar at a wide age-range day/boarding school. In retirement, he is a director of AGBIS; a foundation governor of his local Church of England infant school; a governor of an IAPS preparatory school; and a trustee of the Ramblers Holidays Charitable Trust.

John Deakin is a partner in the Pastoral Department at Veale Wasbrough Vizards. He advises independent schools on a wide range of education and pastoral care issues, including the parent contract and associated agreements, policies and procedures, preparation for inspection and pupil and parent disciplinary matters. He is a regular speaker at conferences and seminars. He is also a former Olympic and world champion coxswain.

Bruno Delacave has been Bursar and Development Director of Norwich School since September 2005. After 12 years with Ernst & Young as a chartered accountant in London, then as a member of their corporate advisory and mergers and acquisitions practices in London, Geneva and New York, he left to be CFO of an investment company in Geneva, before moving to London in 1999 as CFO of an interactive TV company owned by Sky, BT, Panasonic and HSBC. He was then appointed Finance Director of an AIM listed venture capital company before becoming Bursar of Gresham's School. He is a member of the Charity Finance Directors' Group (CFDG) and was elected to the ISBA executive committee in 2009.

Rt Hon Stephen Dorrell PC MP has been Chairman of the Trustees of Uppingham School (where he was a pupil) since 2008 and a member of the Board since 1988. Currently Chairman of the Parliamentary Health Select Committee, he was Secretary of State for National Heritage and then for Health in the John Major government of 1992-7, and has held a wide variety of portfolios both in government and opposition, including education, energy and as Financial Secretary to the Treasury.

Dr Kenneth Edwards was Vice Chancellor of the University of Leicester 1987-99, having been successively Head of the Department of Genetics and Secretary General of the Faculties at Cambridge University. He joined the governing body of the Perse School, Cambridge, in 2001, becoming Chairman a year later. During his seven years in this role he oversaw a substantial increase in the size of the school and a £3m fundraising campaign. He is a former Chairman of CVCP (the Committee of Vice Chancellors and Principals: now Universities UK), and of CRAC. He has also been a visiting lecturer, honorary degree recipient and consultant at many universities both in the UK and abroad.

Gerald Ellison has been Bursar at the Perse School, Cambridge, since 1997. Educated at two independent schools and Keble College, Oxford, he was a finance director and company secretary in civil engineering and horticulture companies until he first became a school bursar in 1991. Recent external work includes bursar appraisal and reviewing bursarial and administrative structures in independent schools, and leading a seminar on project and change management for maintained sector business managers. Other roles include recognised bursarial adviser for ISI inspections; book reviewer for HMC's *Conference & Common Room* magazine; mentor for new bursars; and school governor. He contributed to the earlier volume in this series on senior management teams.

Stephen Fisher has over 12 years experience working with charities and not for profit organisations, the last six of them with haysmacintyre chartered accountants and tax advisers based in Holborn, central London, whose clients include over 100 independent schools and key educational sector governing bodies and professional associations. Stephen trained as a chartered accountant with Deloitte and subsequently gained the ICAEW Diploma in Charity Accounting whilst with haysmacintyre. A qualified teacher and experienced lecturer and facilitator, he is also a trustee and former honorary treasurer of Volunteer Centre Westminster.

Sue Freestone has been Head of the King's School Ely since 2004. Her path to headship was on unusual one: having graduated from the Royal Academy of Music in 1976, her first post was that of Director of Music at North Foreland Lodge. She ran music departments, with a short break to produce two children, for 20 years. Having completed an MEd in educational management at Bristol University, she became Head of Sibford School in Oxfordshire in January 1997. She was Chairman of SHMIS (the Society of Heads of Independent Schools) in 2002.

7

Peter Goddard is an Assistant Head at Norwich School, with particular responsibility for compliance and outreach. He has previously been head of geography, a housemaster and the senior master at the school. He taught at Ryde School, Isle of Wight, before moving to Norwich. He is the author of a number of geography revision texts for schools, the most recent being published in April. He sits on the ISC community committee.

David Goucher was Bursar of Bryanston from 1987 to 1996. After school education at Netherthorpe Grammar School, Chesterfield, he graduated from the RAF College, Cranwell, in 1958. Following a series of other postings, he worked at the RAF Staff College, Bracknell, and the Joint Services Staff College, Latimer, leaving the services as a Group Captain and having been Commanding Officer, RAF Uxbridge, from 1982-3. He was a member of the ISBA committee in 1995-6 and a regular contributor to *Conference & Common Room* in the 1990s.

Richard Green is Deputy Chairman of AGBIS. A chartered accountant and former partner of a constituent firm of Ernst & Young, he has held a number of appointments as finance director, CEO and chairman in a wide range of businesses, including Dunhill, Breguet Watches and Stapletons Tyres. He was until recently a non-executive director of Chelsea Building Society. In the not-for-profit sector, he was Chairman of governors of Royal Russell School, Croydon, for 11 years, and now holds a similar position at Prior's Field School, Godalming. He is also a director of First Wessex, one of the largest housing associations in South-East England.

Hugh Monro read economics and history at Cambridge before working in the tin-making industry. He then taught in England, Scotland and the United States, before being Head of four independent schools (Worksop College, Clifton College, Wellington College and Bristol Cathedral School). He became the founding Principal of the first choir school in the country to become an academy. In 2009, with two other retired Heads, he formed Head-to-Heads, which helps schools to recruit and appraise Heads. He has been involved in the founding of several schools abroad.

Barney Northover is a partner and head of the education and charities practice at law firm Veale Wasbrough Vizards. He advises independent schools on good governance, strategic review, structural change, mergers and charity law. He has an economics degree from Durham University and converted to law at the University of Exeter, after which he joined VWV as a trainee in 1999. The independent legal directory *Chambers and Partners* advises that he 'offers calm, practical advice at times when everyone is under immense pressure' and he also has experience of the governors' perspective, having been a governor of two schools

Ian Power has been Membership Secretary of HMC since 2009. He read natural sciences at Cambridge, specialising in physics, before starting his teaching career at Aylesbury Grammar School. He subsequently moved first to The King's School, Worcester, and then to Millfield, where he ran the physics and science departments respectively, and was a housemaster in two senior houses. He was Headmaster of Lord Wandsworth College for 12 years before moving to his current position, and was Chairman of SHMIS in 2008. He has served on both the ISC and ISI Boards.

Joy Richardson is Vice Chairman of the Trustees at Uppingham School and chairs the education committee there. She is also a governor of a state primary school. After reading history at Cambridge she worked in primary schools and teacher training and now leads inspections for ISI and Ofsted. She has carried out school evaluations in Asia and America and has wide experience of working with governors and school leaders, and contributing to training programmes. She has also been a governor of Monkton Combe School and St John's College School, Cambridge.

Dr Nigel Richardson was Chairman of HMC in 2007 and has been co-editor of all the books in this series. He was Head of the Perse School, Cambridge, 1994-2008, after posts at Uppingham, the Dragon School, Oxford and the King's School, Macclesfield. An appraiser of Heads and teachers, a governor of several HMC schools and a Syndic of the Cambridge University Press, he edited the HMC magazine *Conference & Common Room* from 1999-2002. He has written history

9

books for children and training literature for the Industrial Society, and is working on a biography of the great Victorian Headmaster, Edward Thring.

David Sewell heads up haysmacintyre's work with schools (see Stephen Fisher, above), which he has been advising for over 20 years. His client base also includes related organisations, religious and a variety of other charities. He is actively involved in audit and related financial services, including addressing boards of trustees on governance, financial monitoring and public benefit issues, and he co-ordinates the firm's services on specialist subjects such as employment taxes, commercial trading and VAT. He is a regular speaker at sector conferences and he writes for various publications. He is a governor of an independent boarding school and trustee of a medical relief charity.

Chris Tongue had 20 years as an independent school Head, the last 12 at St John's School, Leatherhead. He read engineering at Cambridge; then taught in the UK and Africa where, at various stages, he was head of department; housemaster; coached sport at first team level; performed in choirs and orchestras and directed drama. He chaired the HMC professional development sub-committee and directed the training courses for new HMC Heads. Post retirement, he has assisted numerous schools with headship and other senior leadership appointments and helped to establish the education wing of CfA (Charity and Fundraising Consultants), an executive search and selection agency specialising in the charitable sector. He has been a regular appraiser of Heads, and is a governor of four schools.

Dr Alan Weeds spent his research career at the Medical Research Council Laboratory of Molecular Biology where he was Director of Studies for a number of years. He also carried out research at Harvard Medical School, Dartmouth Medical School and Stanford Medical School and was a visiting lecturer at Bristol University for ten years. A teaching Fellow in Biochemistry at Trinity College, Cambridge, from 1975-2007, he was for nearly 20 years Senior Director of Studies in Natural Sciences. He was Trinity's appointed governor at the Perse School from 1982-2011 and served as vice chairman from 1995-2011. He was a Trustee Director of the MRC Pension Fund for seven years and continues as a member of the investment subcommittee.

Stuart Westley became general secretary of AGBIS in September 2009. After attending Lancaster Royal Grammar School, he read law at Corpus Christi College, Oxford; then, after a brief, unspectacular spell as a professional cricketer, he taught mathematics at Framlingham College 1973-84 where he was also a Housemaster and Director of Studies. He was subsequently Deputy Head of Bristol Cathedral School 1984-89; Principal of King William's College, Isle of Man, 1989-96 and Master of Haileybury 1996-2009. He is a governor of an HMC school and Chairman of governors of two preparatory schools.

Introduction

Nigel Richardson

This is the eighth and final volume in the *Leading Schools* series – a sequence of books that has focused on the work of Heads; senior management teams; heads of department; newly qualified teachers; those involved in pastoral work; public relations, marketing and development and, mostly recently bursars and their teams. The involvement of John Catt Educational Ltd as publisher, and of HMC (the Headmasters' and Headmistresses' Conference) as co-sponsor, has been a continuing feature of the series.

This book is co-sponsored by AGBIS (the Association of Governing Bodies of Independent Schools). Its member schools are drawn from all the major independent school associations, and it supports and advises them on all aspects of governance. It is schools, rather than individuals, that are members of AGBIS, although its usual points of contact with schools are via chairmen and/or bursars (especially if the latter is also clerk to the governors). Chapter 19 describes some of the range of benefits and advice that it can offer.

As with previous books in this series, contributions have been edited with a fairly light touch – more with house style in mind than in an attempt to eliminate all areas of overlap.

As the opening chapters explain, governance is now more demanding and more multi-faceted than in days gone by – the result of a mixture of political, legislative, financial and social pressures. Successive writers then explore how schools can ensure that they are well prepared for the many challenges that they face by making sure that they have appropriate committee and other structures in place, before the final chapters deal with some specific situations that may arise, and the support which AGBIS can give to governing bodies. At the end we have also included a list of chapter headings from earlier titles in the series, for readers who wish to explore some other topics in depth.

I am very grateful to Stuart Westley, General Secretary of AGBIS, for his advice and editorial help, as well as for his own contributions to the text. The publication of this book comes shortly after the retirement of Geoff Lucas, General Secretary of HMC for a decade, whose moral and practical support for the entire series cannot be overstated; nor can that of Derek Bingham, Publishing Director at JCEL. I am greatly in their debt.

People often observe that the pace of change in society seems to accelerate remorselessly, and education is an extreme example of the maxim that nothing remains constant. As a result, despite our best efforts to avoid going into detail that may become dated, some of the detailed information may be supplanted by new developments during the lifetime of this book. If in doubt, governors should seek expert advice.

However, we hope that the chapters that follow will inform; challenge; sometimes cause you to disagree and above all make you think – and that you will enjoy them and benefit from them. I make no apology for repeating what I wrote in the introduction to Volume 7 (which was concerned with the work of bursars):

> We should never lose sight of the fact that whilst it may take many decades to build up the plant, personnel and reputation of a great school, if its finances, fabric and legal responsibilities are neglected, it may well take only a very short time to close it down.

Governors, as well as a school's senior management, have a crucial role in ensuring that our schools continue to thrive.

Chapter 1

Responsibilities and accountabilities: an overview

Stuart Westley

In the 1940s the governing bodies of boys' and girls' 'public schools' formed two associations, the Governing Bodies' Association (GBA) and the Governing Bodies of Girls' Schools Association (GBGSA). Those associations ran roughly in parallel. The objects of each were to advance education in the independent sector by discussing matters of policy and practice; giving advice to schools in membership; considering their relationship with the wider community and taking action as necessary in the interest of their members. The two Associations merged in June 2002 to form the Association of Governing Bodies of Independent Schools (AGBIS).

Since the merger, AGBIS has welcomed a growing number of preparatory and other schools into its membership. This currently numbers 740 and is increasing by about 20 schools per year. AGBIS continues to support and advise governing bodies of schools in the independent sector, and the objects of the Association are the advancement of education in independent schools and the promotion of good governance in such schools: in other words little changed from those of its forerunners.

This might seem to suggest merely a continuing, gentle evolution, over a period of 70 years or so, of the nature of the work of the governors of our schools, the responsibilities involved and the commitment required. In fact nothing could be further from the truth. In recent years there has been a dramatic increase in the awareness of the magnitude of governors' responsibilities. This in turn has led to much greater attention being paid to the importance of recruitment of suitable people; the range of skills required of governing bodies; the acceptance of the need for thorough induction of new governors; continuing training for new and experienced board members and systematic review of the performance of governing bodies.

The bewildering pace of change

All this takes place against a background of profound and accelerating social, educational and other changes over the past seven decades, all of them profoundly affecting work done in schools. They include the earlier onset of puberty and the foreshortening of childhood; the impact of the internet and social networking on young people; the growth of a child-centred approach to education; less consensus on religious and ethical matters; a less hierarchical and accepting approach to authority and discipline; the rise of the parent and pupil as client or consumer (one of the results of school league tables); a greater emphasis in inspections on learning rather than on top-down teaching; pastoral challenges and expectations of teachers stemming from the breakdown of traditional family patterns in society; growing practical pressures on families from the impact of two working parents; financial pressures arising from the economic crisis; the impact of university tuition fees; a much greater recognition of special educational needs, and ceaseless curriculum and public exam change.

Meanwhile successive governments have looked to schools to fulfil many of the roles played in earlier times by parents, the church and other agencies. Politicians and lawyers demand a growing range of policies and procedures. Schools can sometimes find themselves on the receiving end of displaced stress or frustration from parents, either at parents' evenings or via email. Governors may find themselves dealing, directly or indirectly, with the fall-out from many of these trends.

Good training leads to good governance

Evidence of the growing awareness and importance of the role of governing bodies is not hard to find. Between 2009 and 2010 the number of on-site training courses mounted by AGBIS increased by 100%, while attendance at the eight training seminars increased by 30%. In October 2010, sensing the demand for training, and conscious that many governors lead busy lives which preclude regular attendance at training seminars,

AGBIS introduced an electronic learning course for governors of member schools, intending that the beneficiaries should primarily be new recruits. In reality, that new training opportunity has so far proved just as popular with experienced governors. In less than a year over 500 governors have accessed the course, which consists of four discrete topics.

The second chapter of this programme is currently being prepared. Like the first, it will address four topics. The observations of those governors who have so far accessed the electronic course have been largely favourable regarding both content and ease of navigability. The course is available to governors of member schools at no additional cost simply by downloading from the AGBIS website the registration form, completing and returning it to the office following which a unique password is provided.

Meanwhile, although still a small organisation, AGBIS is acutely conscious of the need to advance communication with individual governors, primarily to provide timely information about governors' substantial responsibilities and the training opportunities available to help them. This publication, in which AGBIS acknowledges with gratitude its partnership with the Headmasters' and Headmistresses' Conference (HMC), is a key element in the continuing mission to inform, support and encourage those who give so generously of their time and talent to the service of our schools.

As to why there has been such an increase in the awareness of governors' responsibilities and the need for training, one suspects that there would be a fairly common view. Against a background of steadily increasing consciousness of responsibility, including legal responsibility, in all walks of life and the consequent need for preparation and training, there has recently been superimposed the recollection of some well publicised, consequential recent events impinging on our schools. Three of the latter come readily to mind.

Legislation and compliance
In 2006, the Office of Fair Trading (as it then was) investigated some 50 independent schools which were found to have exchanged price-sensitive information contrary to competition law. Nobody involved in

that experience would wish to go there again; there was a stark lesson for all to learn, including a clear illustration of governors' unavoidable responsibility for the acts of others.

The Charity Commission's guidance concerning public benefit, recently the subject of judicial review (see chapter 5), can hardly have left any governor of a school which is a charity – which the majority of British independent schools are – unaware of the importance of meeting the obligations which fall to charity trustees. Finally the concern to safeguard the welfare of children entrusted into the care of schools has led to extensive, detailed regulation of both maintained and independent schools – of which, more later.

Here we will simply note that ensuring compliance with that raft of regulation requires the most conscientious attention to detail and a considerable willingness to adapt traditional practices. That protection of children and ensuring their safety is the priority in all circumstances is beyond debate. Responsibility for ensuring compliance unquestionably falls to the proprietor – that is, the governors – and failure to comply understandably can have very serious consequences. Little surprise, therefore, that recent years have seen such a surge in the demand for training in understanding governors' responsibilities.

Independent schools: variety and isolation
Contemplating the training needs of governors quickly leads to two very conspicuous characteristics of Britain's independent schools: their diversity and their isolation. The schools represented within the eight constituent member associations of the Independent Schools Council range in pupil numbers from just over 30 to around 3000. Consideration of their other characteristics – urban/rural, boarding/day, girls/boys/ co-educational, highly selective/non-selective, specialist/non-specialist, denominational/non-denominational, junior/senior/sixth-form-only – indicates just how diverse those schools are and what richness that diversity brings to the sector. But however dramatic the schools' differences are, the responsibilities of their governors – technically referred to as proprietors – are virtually identical. From that point of view what is an issue for one school may well be an issue for all.

Isolation, however, points in the opposite direction. Many, perhaps most, of the governors of our schools will have considerable interest in one school, and occasionally in two or three. For some, the connection will have been of long duration; for others it will be recent. But for almost all of them the interest will be deep and genuine: perhaps even approaching affection.

However, most governors will inevitably have almost no knowledge of the affairs of other schools and often, understandably, little interest in their operation. Thus their knowledge of the challenges other schools face; the mistakes they may make; how they respond to those situations and what they learn in the process remains largely hidden from view, and those very few who *do* know something are expected to remain discreet.

In parallel with this, while some come to governance with valuable experience of the corporate world, much of which will be relevant and transferable to the governance of schools, others will have little or no knowledge of the crucial, essential principles of sound governance. In a good governing body, given self-awareness and discernment, many will learn quickly, and they will learn even more quickly if fellow governors (the Chairman and the clerk particularly) are conscientious over their induction and training.

If in doubt, seek advice

However, by no means all governing bodies are well run. Very occasionally some well-publicised incident highlights obviously poor governance. More commonly, governing bodies are unaware of the principles of good governance; unconscious of good practice; sometimes trapped in their own world of a philosophy of 'this is the way we have always done things here and we think we know best'.

On what authority do we offer advice or training? In the minority of cases the advice has a straightforward justification in law. The law, in some form, requires that you do this, or that you refrain from doing that. That is the end of the matter, and where there is any doubt charity trustees should always seek advice. Some situations are obvious: to any siren voice crying 'I do not wish to keep a central record of appointments or produce an annual set of accounts in the standard form', there is a very short, simple response.

More commonly the issue at stake is a matter of good practice rather than legalities, calling for experience, wisdom, and sometimes humility. This publication, to which a variety of experienced practitioners have very kindly contributed their time and knowledge, aims to share experience; to advise and suggest rather than to instruct. However, it would be hard to argue with the view that the advice and experience offered herein is substantial and enlightened.

For some decades AGBIS and its forebears have published the well-known, respected *Guidelines for Governors,* which proclaims itself to be a manual of good practice. This publication aims to be a little more informal and perhaps rather more anecdotal. Its purpose is to complement and expand on *Guidelines*, not to replace it. However, the two publications have a shared purpose: to support governors; to enable them better to understand their responsibilities and, together with the outstanding executive leadership in our schools, to ensure that in the constant quest for improvement our schools remain the envy of the world. That quest should be a joy, not a burden.

Chapter 2

Legal responsibilities

Barney Northover

In my experience as a lawyer advising a great many schools, the importance of the part played by governors in enabling the independent school sector to continue to provide outstanding educational opportunities to children should not be underestimated. A school's governors are likely to be less visible to its parents, its pupils and the wider school community than its Head and the teaching staff, but it is the governors who are ultimately responsible for the all important decisions about the appointment of the Head and senior management team, and for the wider strategic direction of the school.

The role of governors is not always easy. They are expected to devote a significant amount of time and attention to their school, often while balancing demanding jobs and family commitments. Yet in return they receive no payment and are all too often not appreciated for the essential role they perform. They will often also inherit a culture and ethos which may have developed over many centuries and which makes the school what it is. Maintaining that, while also looking to the future, is a challenge in itself.

The governors' role
If they fail in their legal duties and responsibilities, governors will be held to account and criticised externally by regulators; internally by the Head and bursar; and also by parents at times of change or crisis. In the worst case scenario, if they get things wrong, they can be faced with personal liability.

What follows could be read as a lawyer's list of reasons *not* to act as a governor. That is certainly not the intention (and many of my firm's lawyers act as governors in their time away from work). Fundamentally, good schools need good governors – and good governors can offer a range of experience in many different disciplines (from finance to marketing to maximising educational attainment), often at a very high level. The role is both interesting and rewarding. However, good governors must understand what it is they are responsible for, and the legal and regulatory framework within which they must operate.

Independent schools are not regulated by the Department for Education to the same extent as state-funded schools. Instead, they are regulated by their governing instrument; the policies of their governors; their procedures and practices; their contracts with parents and a number of legal regimes which apply because of the way in which the school operates.

Governors are therefore ultimately responsible for directing the affairs of the school and ensuring that it complies with all its relevant legal obligations, including the law which relates to charities, child protection, companies, competition, construction, consumer credit, education, employment, data protection, discrimination, health and safety, intellectual property, planning and transport.

The governors' duties
Governors' legal obligations derive from the role they perform. Schools are constituted in a variety of ways, but most governors will have several distinct but overlapping roles, being:

- A governor, with the general responsibilities of that position, relating mainly to good practice, knowing, understanding and upholding the ethos and culture of the school and giving proper support to its Head and other members of the senior management team;
- where the school is a company, a director (for the purposes of company law);
- where the school is a charity, a charity trustee, with responsibility for protection of the assets of the school and ensuring that all decisions are taken solely in the school's best interests;
- a member of the proprietor body of the school for the purposes of education and discrimination law; and
- often, also a member of the school for the purposes of company law, with the right to call and attend general meetings if it becomes

necessary to exercise control over the affairs of the school, or for other purposes.

These roles are most extensive where the school is a charity (and the remainder of this chapter is written on the basis that most schools do have charitable status; for non-charitable schools, the duties of governors will be less extensive). As charity trustees, the governors have a duty to act in its best interests. The most significant aspects of this are the obligations to act within the charity's objects and powers, and the duty to act personally. There are also duties to act without conflict of interest and without personal benefit.

The objects of any school are what it was set up to do. They define what it can, and should, do. The powers define how it can pursue its objects. The objects and express powers will be set out in the charity's governing instrument. Additionally, governors have statutory and common law powers available under charity law. To the extent that they don't conflict with charity law, the governors of an incorporated school (*ie* a company or a Royal Charter body) are able to rely on powers conferred by company law in addition to charity law. The governors of an unincorporated charity (*ie* established by a trust or a Charity Commission scheme) must rely on the powers conferred by trust and charity law.

A charitable independent school will often hold assets on particular trusts (*eg* endowment property) or for particular purposes (*eg* bursary or scholarship funds restricted for particular purposes) in addition to its 'corporate' assets. Sometimes a school's site is held on endowment trusts. All of this means that governors need to take great care to ensure that they are exercising the correct powers for the correct purposes when they are dealing with the school's assets, particularly where they are selling or charging property.

In most cases, acting outside their powers (in legal terms, acting *ultra vires*) will be a breach of trust by the governors. A breach of trust can be very serious, because acts or omissions which cause loss to the school (or any of its endowment or restricted trusts) and which are in breach of the governors' duty to the school may lead to personal liability for them. In other words, the governors could be required to put the school back into the position it would have been in had the breach of trust not occurred.

The governors' duty is, first, to exercise such care and skill as is reasonable in the circumstances. The level of care and skill is assessed in the light of an individual governor's knowledge and expertise – so, for example, there is a higher duty in relation to financial matters if a governor is a financial professional.

While a school's incorporation as a charitable company or Royal Charter body will generally protect its governors from personal liability to third parties, it does not protect them from liability for breaches of trust. A liability arising from a breach of trust is owed to the school itself, so the fact that it may be incorporated is irrelevant.

Where the governors of a school act in breach of trust, personal liability is joint and several among the governors; in other words, even if one governor did not act in breach of trust him or herself, but stood by and let someone else sanction something they shouldn't have agreed to, that governor can still find himself personally liable for the breach.

Having said all this, governors should not assume that their role will inevitably lead to bankruptcy and destitution. Instances of personal liability are very rare, particularly because most governors are aware of the risks and put appropriate controls in place to prevent breaches of trust ever happening. Governors can also be excused from personal liability by the Court or the Charity Commission if they conclude that a governor has acted honestly and reasonably and ought fairly to be excused.

One way for governors to protect both themselves and the school is to ensure that they take professional advice (or seek advice from the Charity Commission) on any area about which they are in doubt. Governors who act on the advice of the Commission or a professional adviser will generally be protected from personal liability.

Another approach is to put in place insurance to indemnify the governors against personal liability. It used to be the case that there needed to be express authority in the governing instrument or from the Charity Commission for a charity to pay the premiums on trustee indemnity insurance. This has now changed and governors have a statutory power to take out insurance. However, the permitted extent of the insurance cover is limited to accidental breaches of trust and breaches of the duty of care, and governors cannot be covered if they act dishonestly or recklessly.

Other than a breach of trust, governors may be made personally liable for the liabilities owed by the school to third parties, *eg* to the charity's employees, contractual counterparties or creditors. The scope for a liability of this kind arising will vary, depending on whether the school is incorporated or unincorporated.

There is an offence of corporate manslaughter which arises where the way in which an organisation's senior managers manage or organise its activities causes a person's death, but this offence relates to the culpability of an organisation as a whole and governors cannot be held individually liable.

A governor can, however, face individual liability for manslaughter if a jury finds that he or she has committed the common law offence of manslaughter. However, prosecutions of directors or governors for common law manslaughter are extremely rare, and only arise if a jury finds that a person has caused death through gross negligence and has had such disregard for the life of the deceased that the governor's conduct should be seen as criminal and deserving of punishment.

Delegation

The second aspect of the duty to act in the best interests of the school is the duty to act personally. This is a principle originally drawn from the law which regulates private trusts and, on the face of it at least, would require any trustee (including a school governor) to discharge their duties personally: in other words, to manage the school's operations day to day.

Clearly, a school's governors cannot be expected to do everything in relation to a school themselves. The law allows them to delegate their powers to others, as must be the case in order to allow a complex operating entity such as a school to function properly. The important point for the school's governors is that they cannot ultimately delegate their responsibilities as charity trustees. The proverbial buck stops with them.

The governors are not therefore 'executives'. Their role is more akin to the non-executive directors of a private or public company. A Head once suggested to us that a better analogy can be found in football, with the Head managing a team of teachers whose goal is education under the overall supervision of a board of directors. The parents are presumably the fans, with all that this implies in terms of the ability simultaneously to support and criticise their team.

Different schools manage delegation in different ways. Some governors delegate all their executive powers to the Head and authorise further delegation from him or her. Others delegate to both the Head and the bursar. There is no standard model for this – each school creates, or lapses into, its own dynamic. Factors that influence the way delegation works within a school (and therefore the dynamics between the governors and the senior management team) typically include:

- Whether too much business is referred to the full governing body for decision instead of report – this can lead to too many governors' meetings, or not enough time for governors to consider important strategic issues.
- Whether enough – or too much – authority is given to the finance and general purposes committee.
- The skills and ability of the Head and the bursar and the working relationships between themselves and with the governors.

Some delegation will be partial only, in the sense that it is guided by a committee of the governors, but every delegation is a delegation of power and not a delegation of responsibility. If there is an insufficient understanding by governors of their powers and responsibilities, this may lead to an over-cautious and defensive approach to governance and a tendency to become risk averse. In our experience this can, over the longer term, mean that governors fail to respond to change in an appropriate way, resulting in the failure of the school to develop and thrive.

Conversely, it may lead to a wish to be hands-on and to get involved with executive decision making (to use the footballing analogy, for the club's directors to dictate to the manager who he should play and where). Delegation implies a duty to supervise and hold the Head and senior management team accountable for the running and management of the school, but governors should resist the desire to interfere in day-to-day management, which can be very de-motivating for the senior management team, and may ultimately restrict the school's ability to develop.

It is important, therefore, that the scope and extent of what is delegated to whom and by whom is clearly considered and articulated. In practice, we see problems arise where roles and responsibilities are not clearly understood, sometimes leading to unnecessary conflict between the governors and senior management team.

The best way to prevent this happening is to have a written scheme of delegation which is consistent with the school's governing instrument and which prescribes not only the scope and extent of the delegation to the Head and senior management team, but also the division of responsibilities and tasks between them. It is also important to keep both the scheme of delegation and the school's governing instrument up to date with charity and company law and also good governance practice in schools and the wider charitable sector.

Strategy and accountability

One of the most important responsibilities of a school's governors is to set the strategic direction of the school. They need to find the right balance between continuing and promoting the traditions, culture and ethos of the school and developing the school so that it grows and changes with the times. Discharging this responsibility will involve reviewing and understanding the school's position in the market and ensuring that its business model allows it to remain sustainable, not only for current pupils but also for future generations of pupils, with the ability to generate surpluses for investment.

Where successive generations of governors get the strategic part of their role right, they are unlikely to be recognised for their work to the extent that they deserve. Where they do not, the likelihood is that it is the governors who will be held to account and criticised by the external and internal groups already described.

The remainder of this chapter deals with accountability in a little more detail. However, it is worth mentioning that, in our experience, parents and perhaps some staff often have a limited understanding of the role of the governors and the variety of different constituencies to whom they are accountable. Parents are understandably interested primarily in their children's education. They are likely to be much less aware of the financial and regulatory constraints that the governors must deal with day to day, let alone the school's longer term strategic requirements.

Parents and staff are entitled to know, in general terms, why a particular state of affairs exists. They are not entitled to know the detail of discussions at governors' meetings. For example, the school may be in a difficult financial position, although the governors have realistic plans for recovery over several years.

Information of that kind, other than that which is required to be published annually, must normally be kept confidential by governors so as not to destabilise the school and detract from its work. The governors are also responsible for keeping confidential any private information concerning parents, pupils and staff – other than to the extent that disclosure is required or permitted by law.

Staff

The governors are responsible for recruiting and appointing the Head of the school. The bursar is often also appointed by the governors. Although much of the day-to-day administration of the school is delegated to the Head and senior management team, the governors are responsible for appointing the right team and for managing its performance. The management team is, in turn, authorised to manage the school's other staff.

The recruitment of all staff (and any volunteers) should comply with the rules on safer recruitment, employment and discrimination which apply from time to time and it is the role of the governors to ensure that authority is properly delegated in a way which ensures that appropriate compliant systems and policies are in place.

HR compliance has become an increasing burden on schools in recent years. There has been a significant increase in the number of schools which engage HR professionals to manage legal compliance, from the employment contract to all the policies and procedures which are required to minimise the risks of employment law liability. Likewise, with a more demanding inspection regime and a requirement to maintain a single central register of pre-employment checks now instituted, governors should ensure that appropriate systems and resources are in place. Checks are also required on the governors and should be recorded in the single central register.

Having delegated authority for the management of staff to the Head and senior management team, governors may be required to hear appeals arising from, for example, disciplinary, capability and grievance decisions (see chapter 13). This is an opportunity for the governors to consider whether procedures have been properly followed, and whether fair and reasonable decisions have been made. The procedures should not be overly prescriptive in relation to who should hear an appeal, but this is often done by a sub-committee of three governors.

Governors will want to be regularly informed about staff issues and to take an interest in the proper career development and progression of staff. This will be an important guide to the morale of staff at any particular time and will assist in identifying problems which may not be apparent so readily, because of the inevitable distance between the governors and the day-to-day operation of the school.

Parents and pupils

A school's contract for educational services (the parent contract) is unique in that it is made between the proprietor of the school (*eg* a company or Royal Charter body or, in the case of an unincorporated school, the governors themselves) and parents for the benefit of a third party: the pupil. The pupil is not typically a party to the contract. The terms of the parent contract are generally non-specific about the educational services that the parents are purchasing. Nonetheless, the school will have a range of duties implied or expressed in the parent contract which include, but are not limited to:

- ensuring the educational services are delivered with reasonable skill and care;
- creating and maintaining an environment in which the pupil's safety, welfare and health are safeguarded;
- ensuring that a broad and varied curriculum is properly resourced and staffed;

- maintaining the ethos and culture of the school so that it delivers what the parents believe they have bargained for;
- acting as a review body to consider complaints or reviews of a decision by the Head to expel or remove a pupil permanently from the school; and
- consulting and notifying parents of proposed changes which would impact significantly on the pupil's education or welfare. In practice, much of this will be delegated to the Head and senior management team, but overall responsibility for meeting these duties will remain with the governors.

As the traditional family unit evolves into ever more complex domestic arrangements, it is becoming increasingly difficult for a school to ascertain what information it is obliged to provide to parents who are divorced or separated. Parental entitlement to information may arise under the parent contract, if he or she is a party to it, or by way of his or her 'parental responsibility' under section 2 Children Act 1989.

Wherever possible the school should obtain the agreement of the parents or a copy of a court order setting out the information that each of the parents is to receive about themselves or their child's education.

In addition to the contractual duties and obligations owed to parents, the school will owe a duty of care to the pupil while s/he is in its care. The duty owed to the pupil is to take reasonable steps to anticipate and deal appropriately with foreseeable risks of harm. If the school falls below the reasonable standard of care, giving rise to personal injury or damage to property, a pupil may have a claim against the school in negligence.

Governors are also responsible for ensuring that the school's policies and procedures comply with the required standards and regulations applicable from time to time and that its admissions procedures are non-discriminatory. A claim for discrimination may arise if a prospective pupil is found to have suffered less favourable treatment because of a certain 'protected characteristic' as defined in the Equality Act 2010.

Protected characteristics include disability, race, gender, gender reassignment, religious belief, pregnancy, maternity and sexual orientation. There is an exemption for single-sex schools, and selective schools may admit pupils on academic grounds – but they must make reasonable adjustments to accommodate disabled candidates who attend for entrance tests or interviews at the school.

Regulators

Governors are accountable to a number of different regulators and have a number of reporting and accounting obligations. While the bursar will generally undertake the work involved in preparing the school's report and financial statements, final responsibility for ensuring that they are compiled, approved, audited and filed lies with the governors.

Schools constituted as companies are subject to company law and, in particular, the Companies Act 2006. They are also subject to regulation by the Registrar of Companies ('Companies House'). This is mostly a 'light touch' regulatory regime, with the main requirement being an obligation to file an annual return, an annual report and financial statements. The 2006 Act also requires all companies to inform Companies House about certain changes in their constitution, structure and management, and failure to do so within prescribed periods of time can be a criminal offence. Automatic financial penalties are also imposed for a failure to meet the deadlines.

Charitable schools are subject to charity law and, in particular, the Charities Act 2011. As charities, they are regulated by the Charity Commission. In addition to the obligations to file an annual return/ report/statements (which must include a statement in relation to the public benefit provided by the school) with the Commission, certain actions that the school may wish to take may require the Commission's consent. Examples include changing a school's objects; conferring a benefit on a governor where there is no express or statutory power to do so, and disposing of or charging land in certain circumstances.

Governors also have a duty to report to the Charity Commission any serious incidents that arise in the school. These include fraud, theft or the significant loss of funds; the actual, alleged or suspected abuse or mistreatment of a pupil; a failure to put in place and operate child protection policies; governors acting whilst disqualified from being a charity trustee; a criminal investigation into the school; an investigation or the imposition of sanctions by another regulator, or any other incident which represents a serious threat to the school or its pupils, assets or reputation.

A report is also required to the Independent Safeguarding Authority where a member of staff, volunteer, governor or contractor is considered unsuitable to work with children or vulnerable adults or resigns before such a finding could be made. It is a criminal offence to fail to make such a report.

Independent schools are not, for the most part, affected by the Education Acts or directly regulated by the Department for Education (although they are inspected by the Independent Schools Inspectorate under powers delegated by the Secretary of State for Education). However, the governors are responsible for ensuring that the school holds a valid registration on the Register of Independent Schools maintained by the Department for Education and must ensure that all reasonable endeavours are used to comply with the regulatory requirements necessary to keep the registration in place.

The Education Act 2002 and the Education (Independent School Standards) (England) Regulations 2003 (as amended) also require an independent school to publish certain information, policies and documents in order to meet inspection standards.

Schools hold significant amounts of personal information about staff, parents and pupils, much of it 'sensitive' under data protection legislation. A school is required by the Information Commissioner to register as 'data controller' to enable it lawfully to process personal information for the purposes for which it is held. The governors are responsible for ensuring that the registration is correct and that there are proper and robust policies in place for the processing, retention and destruction of personal information.

The majority of independent schools require fees to be paid by parents in advance of each term. A deferment of this condition usually amounts to the school providing consumer credit to the parents. The Consumer Credit Act 1974 (as amended) regulates those who provide such credit. Unless the agreement made with parents falls within an available exemption under the 1974 Act, the school will require a consumer credit licence or risk a fine and possible imprisonment for members of staff.

If a consumer credit agreement is regulated by the 1974 Act, the school must also comply fully with regulations governing pre and post contract matters and must ensure that the agreement is in a format prescribed by the regulations. There is a limited number of external credit providers to whom the school may refer parents. When making such a referral, the school must consider whether this amounts to activity which would require a 'credit brokerage' consumer credit licence.

Charitable schools are able to take advantage of a wide range of reliefs and exemptions from tax (and VAT, although the net effect of exemption from VAT is not always beneficial to the school). Schools are obliged to 'self assess' their liability (if any) to tax and can, in certain circumstances, be obliged to submit a tax return to HM Revenue & Customs. While a school's tax affairs will typically be dealt with by the bursar and his staff, the governors should ensure that they understand the school's obligations, particularly in relation to areas such as PAYE, salary sacrifice and trading activities which are not incidental to the provision of education.

Conclusions

Although much of what a school's governors do may not always be apparent to its parents, pupils and some staff, they are ultimately responsible for the proper running of the school day to day (and, in particular, the welfare of its pupils and staff and safeguarding its assets, finances and reputation) whilst also keeping a firm grip on its longer term strategy and direction of travel.

It is important not to underestimate the vital part played by good governance in ensuring the stability and success of independent schools. In a competitive market, independent schools need to be at the top of their game in all respects, and it is essential to have a strong and well balanced board of governors made up of individuals with the right set of skills and experience who can work well as a team.

Central to this is a clear understanding of the governors' role and responsibilities. If a school is thriving, much of that success will be attributable to good governance. Conversely, poor governance will, sooner or later, damage the school's prospects.

Chapter 3

Health & Safety

Bruno Delacave

Starting any chapter on Health & Safety (H&S) matters might well be one of the best remedies for insomnia. However, the current legislative and operational environment is one in which H&S cannot be ignored and therefore this chapter has an important place in any review of the management of schools. I write as a bursar, but while I am conscious of the difference between management and governance, governors have a key role of oversight in this area – which this chapter will explain.

Everyone has a H&S story to tell, but mine was unfortunately a tragic one. Our school had arranged through a reputable local bus company to take a party of children and staff for a week's holiday abroad. We were unaware that the coach company had been faced with unexpected staffing problems resulting in a driver being allocated to our journey who had not had sufficient rest.

In the depth of a dark winter's night on a continental motorway, the coach driver experienced a micro-sleep as a result of which his reactions were too slow to avoid an accident. A member of our staff was killed, as was the driver's assistant. Our school community was profoundly shocked and mourned the loss of a dear colleague. Then, not too long afterwards, the searching questions started. Whose fault was this? Why did it happen? Who is liable? More helpfully, can we learn anything?

At another end of the spectrum, a surprise inspection by the Health & Safety Executive (HSE) to check our ladder register and storage procedures proved that our attention to detail was good and of a high standard. We were also the subject of another surprise HSE inspection regarding our visitor policies, which looked for proof that unauthorised access to our site was prohibited as far as was reasonably possible. I'm glad that in both cases we met the standards.

However, in another school with only minimal H&S management, I was asked to address teachers about the need for improvements to the school's policies and practices in order to meet at least the minimum legal requirements at that time. "Why do we need this?" responded a teacher, "we hardly have any accidents here!" With that comment, sheep-like, the common room persuaded itself that everything was fine.

H&S is not something that we have choice about, despite the fact that we often feel, in common with many politicians, teachers and businessmen that, in the words of regular newspaper messages, 'health 'n safety' has become excessive. Many would accept that planning, managing, operating and reviewing such issues properly, does lead to a less risky and ultimately safer school. This is particularly important to us: we take responsibility for the care of vulnerable people – namely our pupils – and schools therefore represent an environment that is naturally more risky than others.

At the time of writing (2011-2), it would appear that the coalition government is aware of the excessive extent to which H&S legislation has invaded almost all areas of commercial, social and charitable activity, and certainly everything that a school does. Lord Young noted that school trips were required to prepare a 12-page risk assessment, which was causing many trips to be cancelled through exasperation at what was being demanded by the HSE and associated bodies. While there is clearly a move to redress the excessive burden of red tape, it is European legislation that pushes the UK to have such extensive H&S provisions and this impetus is not likely to reduce in the future. This means that H&S legislation and the associated rules, policies and laws, are here to stay.

What is it all about?
H&S legislation and the formation of HSE to oversee its implementation arose from a desire to reduce the level of injuries and sickness in, and caused by, workplace activities. It is an employer's duty to ensure that it properly adheres to the legislation: most H&S responsibilities land on the employer, which, for a school means that the responsibility for H&S ultimately rests with, and begins with, the governors.

The board as a corporate body has a separate legal identity from its members making them liable as a whole. These facts do not mean that the school's employees are free from responsibility as it is most likely that the governors will want to ensure that every employee of the school has some part to play in establishing a school-wide culture of H&S.

Since the legislation has come into force, HSE proudly states that annual workplace fatalities fell from 650 to 150 in the period from 1974 to 2009 and that the non-fatal injury rate has fallen by more than 50% since 1986. Some of this reduction is due to the changing nature of work. However, there are still 1.3 million people each year suffering from illnesses caused, or made worse, by their work. Nationally, more than 121,000 absences of more than three days were reported in 2010, although research suggests that the actual figure might be even greater.

Although the education sector is noted for being a safe place in which to work (as evidenced by having the third lowest rate of reportable injuries), slips and trips are responsible for one third of accidents. This should be something that schools can limit or control. Despite this relatively benign conclusion, there are also annually one or two fatalities in the education sector and, more worryingly, the rate of mental health illness is almost double the all-industry average. Schools must therefore play their part, both morally and by virtue of legislation, in implementing health and safety policies and procedures.

How should we go about it?

One or more members of the governing body should be allocated the responsibility for reporting to the governors on the school's approach to, and success in, implementing the necessary H&S practices and policies. They will refer to the H&S policy contained within the school's Policy & Procedures manual.

This policy should contain a statement of intent or commitment; a detailed management structure showing responsibilities and a definition of standards for specific hazards or policies. In order to carry out their duties, the governors will want to ensure that they regularly review the policy, with relevant advice from professionals as appropriate. Any relevant governors should receive training in H&S matters, and they should benefit from an extensive H&S induction by the school on being appointed to this role. The induction could contain advice from external professionals; sight of HSE publications and short films; a summary of the H&S history of the school, as well as visits to areas of risk and evidence of H&S procedures in action.

The H&S governor will need to study the management structure contained within the school's H&S policy. It is recommended that the Head has ultimate operational responsibility within the school, assisted by two senior members of staff responsible for H&S, one focusing on the teaching activities within the school and the other on the non-teaching areas. In this way the responsibility is shared: otherwise the demands of H&S can become excessive for one person, especially if the school is a large one. It is also advisable that the school has an internal H&S committee where all teaching and support staff most closely related to areas of risk gather at least twice a term to discuss the school's policy in light of recent events and legislative changes. The committee should include those with responsibility for facilities, boarding, science, art & design, sport, nursing/medical staff, trips and visits the child protection officer(s), and anyone else with responsibility for particular areas of risk within the school environment. Accidents should be regularly reported, and reviewed at these meetings, and minutes should be made available to the school's senior management team, to the governors, and posted to all staff.

In addition to the structure mentioned above, certain departments are expected to comply with specific H&S legislation insofar as it relates to their particular activities such as DATA for design and CLEAPPS for science.

The school, given this structure, will be in a position to define and revise its school-wide H&S objectives. How well the school is doing in achieving them will be communicated regularly to governors, to the senior leadership team and to staff; it helps to build a school-wide culture of risk assessment. It is likely that the school will also wish to establish some key measures that help to define objectively how well H&S is being carried out, including numbers of incidents, costs of delivering

H&S, confirmation that risk assessments and schemes of work are being produced in a comprehensive and timely manner, and the outcome of any external audit of H&S in the school.

How do we know what to do?

The traditional model is to allow certain employees of the school to undertake the necessary research into H&S issues through membership of their professional associations, contacts with colleagues in other schools and reading of the press and other trade publications. Depending on each individual's competence and interest in this work, such an approach can be helpful, but only up to a certain point. It is unlikely that s/he will be able to address legal issues relating to H&S, especially recent cases; s/he won't cover all the areas of the school; it will lead to a fractured approach to H&S across the school; and it will cause over-reliance on a particular individual, which would be particularly difficult if s/he were absent from school. It is therefore recommended that schools combine external professional 'overview' advice with the appointment of a number of employees to have particular responsibility for health and safety in particular areas.

The external advisor should be required to update the school on *all* the relevant H&S issues and this advice should be of a level that the advisor would accept liability if it were to be proved incorrect. A contract between the school and the provider should be required, as should the settling of financial terms and a service level agreement. The external advisor should be well placed to undertake the H&S audit as not only will this permit it to ensure that the school is adopting its recommendations fully, but it will deepen its own understanding of the school's particular issues hence allowing it to make the best recommendations for future action.

The advisor would report to the H&S committee and to the governors. The advantage of this approach is the time and worry many staff have about whether they are doing the right things for H&S will be undertaken by the external advisor; staff can therefore focus on their role of ensuring that the necessary H&S procedures are being properly carried out in the particular areas for which they are responsible.

What should we be doing?

Virtually everything to do with H&S is risk-assessment based, a concept instituted in the *Management of Health and Safety at Work Regulations 1999*. The risk assessments seek to define whether something is inherently risky and, separately, how likely that risk is to arise. Taken together they produce a measure of riskiness about which the school can do something, by taking 'measures' that it considers reasonable in mitigating the risk. Almost everything a school does has risk, which means that risk assessments should exist for the whole gamut of school business. Those carrying out the risk assessments should know how to do them, and the school should have developed a standard, school-wide, risk assessment for every member of staff to use. Certain departments and activities will also have additional risk assessments that relate specifically to their activities such as Control of Substances Hazardous to Health (COSHH), noise, vibration, asbestos, fire, legionella *etc.* All such assessments should be centrally stored, easily accessible to update or refer to, up-to-date and regularly used and referred to.

It is not possible to list every area of risk that a school should risk assess, but some of the common areas in which the Independent Schools Bursars Association (ISBA) regularly provides training for bursars include school trips, swimming pools, fire risk assessments, COSHH, asbestos, manual handling, working at heights, visual display units (VDUs), lone working, slips and trips, workplace transport and stress. Where a school operates boarding houses, these are subjected to specific fire risk assessments under the Fire Safety Order.

The school should also note that where particular activities are regularly performed or specific equipment regularly used that have known hazards associated with them, the school is well advised to established 'schemes of work' that ensure all employees are completely clear about the safe operation of the equipment or activities.

Will it cost us a lot?

The cost associated with H&S is significant and every school should budget accordingly. How much you actually need to spend will depend on your current H&S environment; the extent and proficiency of your existing H&S processes; whether you use external advisers and, above all, on how you have decided to manage the risks in your school.

Nationally it is estimated that H&S activities cost employers in the range of £3.9 to £8.8 billion each year, but costs specific to the education sector are unknown. You will have noted above a number of key steps requiring an investment of time, in professional advice and in systems that should be carefully managed and budgeted for. It would not be unusual, given the time and material costs of such activities, to find that they result in an annual cost for H&S to the school of about 1% of tuition fee income per annum.

Any other advice?

The HSE and the Institute of Directors (IoD) have jointly issued guidance in INDG417 entitled *Leading Health & Safety at Work*, which provides some additional insights into good practice. Visits to other schools always provide useful and meaningful insights. Attendance at training courses, such as the H&S courses run by ISBA, are essential.

Final thoughts

Accidents can and do happen, deeply regrettable though this is. Any school should therefore aim to ensure that it has taken all reasonable measures to mitigate such occurrences and that it fosters a safe culture within the entire school community. A safe school will be one in which staff and pupils flourish; an unsafe one might, in the worst-case scenario, result in death and the governors or school leadership being jailed. Every school has the opportunity to choose to what level it wishes to invest in H&S, but no school can simply opt out and hope for the best. Thus, to return to where I began: governors have an important role in ensuring that their school is fully on top of all its H&S responsibilities.

Chapter 4

Some risk management issues

Health and Safety is only one aspect of the risk that schools face. This chapter describes three other ways in which schools can address the question, and how to manage risk responsibly.

a) The risk register

Sue Freestone

All schools are complex organisations and risk, of one kind or another, is inherent in all we do. As chapter 2 explained, all registered charities with an annual turnover of more than £10,000 are required to report to the Charity Commission every year, and one of the commission's key expectations is that charities demonstrate that risk is managed efficiently. The Charity Commission itself provides exhaustive advice on creating a risk register on its website (www.charitycommission.gov.uk) under 'Charities and Risk Management: a guide for trustees'.

In creating a risk register, schools need to consider not only those risks that present themselves in the daily run of events, but also to consider the wider context in which the school operates. Aspects of this include the vagaries of the financial climate; new legislation; changes in society and its expectations; the natural environment and advances in technology. It is also essential to think the unthinkable, and to put in place a disaster plan in the event of serious damage to school property through fire, flood or vandalism; pandemic, serious IT failure or even terrorism.

The responsibility for the management of risk lies ultimately with trustees and whatever kind of risk register you create, it needs to be ratified regularly by your governing body.

According to the *Charities (Accounts and Reports) Regulations 2008*, charities that are required by law to have their accounts audited must make a risk management statement in their trustees' annual report confirming that '...the charity trustees have given consideration to the major risks to which the charity is exposed and satisfied themselves that systems or procedures are established in order to manage those risks'. Auditors will also expect to see a record of comprehensive risk management and I am grateful to Liz Hazell, Head of Charities at PricewaterhouseCoopers LLP, for the information in the next three paragraphs:

> From an auditor's perspective, a comprehensive risk register provides a good starting point when considering the areas of potential focus for the audit. As a self-assessment tool, the risk register summarises management's and trustees' views of where they consider the organisation is at most risk across a range of different areas. It also gives an indication of what controls are in place to mitigate those risks. How seriously the risk assessment process is taken by an organisation can give a good indication of the tone at the top: an organisation that treats it lightly may indicate one that has a similar approach to its governance, internal controls and systems, thus providing an indicator to the auditor that there might be more risk of error in, for example, financial information.

> Conversely those organisations that think strategically about risk can get real value out of the process. What things might prevent you from achieving your strategy or from performing optimally? The answers would be captured within the risk register but could also be areas of opportunity: a risk register isn't all negative! Logically these questions also help to inform decisions on other areas such as investment strategy, reserves policies, budgeting, cash-flow forecasting and whether the organisation is sustainable in the longer term. When trustees or the auditor consider the concept of 'going concern', as they should before approving the accounts, joined up thinking between these areas is essential.

> For an internal auditor, the risk register is helpful when assessing where to focus audit effort across the organisation, so that the internal

audit plan can be targeted at those areas of greatest risk or where you are most dependent on controls and procedures to mitigate those risks. Trustees and audit committees can then make more informed decisions in guiding the use of this resource. This helps to get the greatest benefit to the organisation, with internal audit complementing the focus of the external auditor, the latter being primarily on the financial reporting in the annual accounts rather than the day to day operations and transactions.

When considering risks, they need to be categorised according to the threat they pose and the likelihood that they will occur. Major risks are those that have a major impact and a probable (or highly probable) likelihood of occurring. If a school is vulnerable to a risk that carries a potentially high impact on its operation, it should be considered and evaluated regardless of how remote the likelihood of the risk becoming a reality.

Risk management policies and their mapping
The first step is to create a risk management policy. This should detail the process to be used in identifying risks and controls, assessing risks and evaluating actions required. In the words of *Charities and Risk Management: A Guide for Trustees, June 2010*: 'An effective charity regularly reviews and assesses the risks it faces in all areas of its work and plans for the management of those risks. The implementation of an effective risk management policy is a key part of ensuring that a charity is fit for purpose.'

One method of setting out the risks faced by your school is in a risk map. The identification of risks should be done by those with a detailed knowledge of the way in which the school operates. While the risk management statement places the responsibility for identifying risks at the door of trustees, input into this process will depend, to a very large extent, on senior staff. Risks posed to and by any wholly owned subsidiary companies should also be taken into account.

Inevitably, risk identification will involve some subjective judgements. Although no process can possibly be exhaustive, it should serve to provide reasonable assurance that all risks have been identified. Risks should be considered under the following broad headings:

- Governance
- Operations
- Finances
- Environmental or external factors including reputational ones
- Compliance

When creating a Risk Map, the most difficult part of this process is identifying all of the threats potentially facing your school. Once that is done, evaluating their likelihood and impact in the context of your school may often be quite clear. Each risk is scored according to the severity of its impact and the likelihood of it happening.

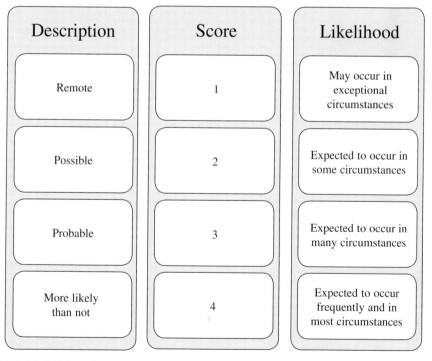

Description	Score	Likelihood
Remote	1	May occur in exceptional circumstances
Possible	2	Expected to occur in some circumstances
Probable	3	Expected to occur in many circumstances
More likely than not	4	Expected to occur frequently and in most circumstances

Risk Likelihood Definitions

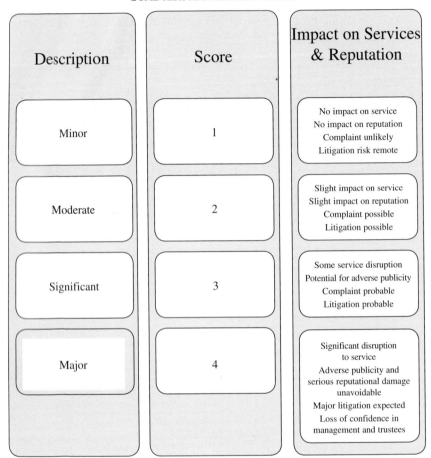

Description	Score	Impact on Services & Reputation
Minor	1	No impact on service No impact on reputation Complaint unlikely Litigation risk remote
Moderate	2	Slight impact on service Slight impact on reputation Complaint possible Litigation possible
Significant	3	Some service disruption Potential for adverse publicity Complaint probable Litigation probable
Major	4	Significant disruption to service Adverse publicity and serious reputational damage unavoidable Major litigation expected Loss of confidence in management and trustees

Risk Impact Definitions

In defining the categories you might use, the following may be of use: The 'heat map' below offers a visual way of demonstrating assessed risk by a scoring of X against Y where X is likelihood and Y is impact. Adding colour to the map will further accentuates the level of risk posed.

Red (dark grey in this illustration) represents major or extreme risks that score 12 or more

44

Yellow (light grey) represents moderate or major risks that score between 6 and 9

Impact	Risk score			
major	4	8	12	16
significant	3	6	9	12
moderate	2	4	6	8
minor	1	2	3	4
Likelihood	remote	possible	probable	more likely than not

Green (no shading) represents minor or insignificant risks scoring 4 or less

Having assessed the risks, the school will need to consider what actions may be required to mitigate any given risk, and, is some cases to recognise that action is required. Risks may take on new weighting in the light of experience and in response to changing external factors and the map will require termly review and amendment.

The table illustration on page 46 offers a few example categories of how the system can be applied. They are only examples (chosen for the fact that they represent varying traffic lights), but a much longer list of categories that might be considered follows the chart. The actions to be taken and the traffic light to be allocated to each category will, of course, vary from school to school

45

Risk Map – Anywhere College- December 2012

	Risk Description	Owner	Likelihood	Impact	Risk Score	Action Plan	Frequency of Review	Date of last review	Action to mitigate risk, or reduce to 'as low as reasonably possible': (alarp)
1	Compliance – Health & Safety	Head (H&S Consultants)	4	4	16	Reviews of each category: contact with professional advisers. Attendance at relevant seminars.	Annually	24ii12	Review by Chairman of Board of Governors
4	Bad debts	Head (School Solicitors)	3	4	12	Routine reports to E & F Committee	Termly	12xi12	Review by Chairman of Exec. and Finance Committee
15	Cash Flow	Head, School Accountant & Director of Finance and Admin/ Bursar	2	4	8	Review of cash flow statements	Termly	12xi12	Review by Chairman of Board of Governors
16	Governors' suitability	Nominations Committee	2	4	8	Careful screening of new Governors	As required		Review Chairman of Board of Governors
56	Staff development	Head	1	3	3	Appraisals and CPD programme	Annually	Continuous	Review by Chairman of Board of Governors
58	Compliance – Data Protection	Head (School Solicitors)	1	2	2	Reviews of each category: contact with professional advisers. Routine attendance at seminars.	Continuous		Review by Chairman of Board of Governors

Finally, here is a longer list of possible risk descriptions which might be included, listed by possible traffic light designations:-

Red	Yellow	Green
Compliance: health and safety	Public perception	Lack of appropriate insurance
Compliance; child protection	Fundraising (lack of)	Reserves
Pandemic event	Child Protection	Asset and investment
Bad debts	Compliance: statutes	management
Trips	Succession planning for Chairman	Corporate protection
Disaster recovery	Succession planning for Head	Governors' personal liability for
	Borrowings/bank relations	sch. Losses/legal action
	Lack of strategic direction	Compliance: employment law
	Cash flow	Resource management
	Governors' suitability	
	Compliance: charities law	
	Professional negligence	
	Fraud or error	
	Security	
	Taxation	
	IT systems	
	Compliance: companies law	
	Staff recruitment/retention	
	Forbidden activities	
	Government policy	
	Loss of revenue	
	Project management	
	Marketing/communications	
	Financial viability (incl. Dev. Projects)	
	Budgetary control	
	Health and safety (various)	
	Fee levels	
	Conflicts of interest	
	Organisational structure	
	Information flow	
	Repairs and maintenance	
	Compliance: equal opportunities/discrimination	
	Compliance: OFT	
	Compliance: fiscal	
	Compliance: European law/statutory reporting	
	Contractual obligations	
	Employment issues	
	Educational trends	

NB: Full versions of sample risk registers can be found on both the AGBIS and ISBA websites.

b) Corporate risk

David Sewell and Stephen Fisher

Where corporate and constitutional risk is concerned, the following is not exhaustive but it focuses on those areas of risk most relevant to schools. Where we refer to governors you can assume that governors are also charity trustees and company directors where relevant. Specific references to trustees or directors refer more generally to the legal or best practice requirements of those offices.

Corporate status

If one were establishing a charitable school now, *unless it is very simple* a company limited by guarantee would be the best legal form. Its advantage arises from the separate legal identity of the company, making it distinct from its directors and allowing it to enter into contracts, sue, be sued and own property in its own name. The school's governors would be the company directors as well as trustees for the purposes of charity law. Unless they act improperly, their personal liability in respect of the company can be limited to the guarantee of a notional amount.

It is still relatively common for older schools to be unincorporated trusts. Contracting and property ownership are more cumbersome as trusts do not have a separate legal identity, although this can be overcome by obtaining a certificate of incorporation under part 12 of the Charities Act 2011. More seriously, an unincorporated trust does not provide the trustees with limited liability.

Other corporate bodies include those incorporated by Royal Charter or, rarely, by special Acts of Parliament. Also, the new Charitable Incorporated Organisation (CIO) now exists in law although the related regulations are outstanding.

Mitigation of governors' liabilities

Governors must, as trustees and/or directors, act in the best interests of the charity. If they fail to do so they are likely to be liable for any losses resulting. With an unincorporated school the governors risk being personally liable for any liabilities the school cannot pay even if they have acted properly.

These significant risks can be mitigated. At the risk of stating the obvious, we should remember the best risk mitigation is for the governors to discharge their duties well and exercise due care and diligence. Relevant tools include a strategic plan and detailed business plans, proper policies, procedures and controls, and realistic budgeting with timely monitoring of the actual figures.

A charity is now legally empowered to purchase indemnity insurance for trustees unless its constitution forbids it. Opinions differ on the usefulness of the policies available. In general it is safe to say that no policy will give trustees *carte blanche* to discharge their duties recklessly and that the detail of any specific policy offered should be closely reviewed in terms of the extent and suitability of the cover, and value for money. An additional factor is that the *absence* of trustees' indemnity insurance may deter some from becoming governors.

For unincorporated schools, incorporation should be seriously considered.

Changes to incorporated status

In principle it is not unduly difficult to move from an unincorporated charity to an incorporated one but a reasonable amount of time and some expense is involved. Schools undertaking this should engage the services of a suitably experienced lawyer. The basic approach is to set up a new charitable company and transfer the school's undertaking to it. Care is needed to ensure that future legacies remain receivable and that no pension deficits crystallise. Also, where a school has a permanent endowment the Charity Commission tends not to allow this to transfer. However, where the endowment is retained in the old charity a Uniting Direction can be obtained so that both the old and new charities are administered together and prepare one aggregated set of accounts.

Corporate trustee

An alternative to the above is to incorporate a company limited by guarantee to be the (sole) trustee of the unincorporated charity. The governors would then be the directors, and usually the members, of this company.

Acting *ultra vires*

As chapter 2 explained, governors are also personally responsible for losses incurred from activities that the school is not legally empowered to undertake. Schools may have restricted objects in terms of the sex or age range of pupils or the location of the activities. Some schools have recently widened their objects to encompass a broader range of public benefit activities. The objects should always be checked whenever any new undertaking is mooted. It is surprising how often this basic step is omitted.

Non-charitable trading

Charity law permits charities to carry out non-primary purpose trading if the activity poses no significant risk to the charity's assets. A trading subsidiary is normally used to carry out those activities when that turnover exceeds £50,000, the small trading exemption from corporation tax. The contractual relationship between the two entities needs to be at arms-length and care is needed with the funding arrangements and to minimise the impact of taxes.

Payments to governors

Unless specifically prohibited by the governing document, governors may claim reasonable expenses incurred in the discharge of their duties.

Trustees may not be paid for fulfilling their role as trustees but they can now be remunerated for providing services unless constitutionally forbidden. Where a governor has expertise in a particular field, that governor may well be the most cost effective source of advice. Such arrangements should be agreed by the Board in advance and this should be recorded. Furthermore, only a minority of governors should be so remunerated.

Management of conflicts of interest

Conflicts of interest will occur. Governors may be parents, trustees of other related bodies, directors of a trading subsidiary or possibly even employees (rare in the independent sector). These situations give rise to conflicts of interest.

Conflicts should be appropriately managed. There should be a written policy that provides for the following: a register of interests; declarations of interests as a standard item at each meeting; the exclusion of a conflicted trustee from relevant decisions; and a definition of those circumstances where a conflicted trustee should be required to step down.

Directors of a charitable company have a legal duty to avoid conflicts of interest. Unavoidable conflicts can be authorised by the other directors if the articles of the company permit. This provision is a recent one so will only exist in schools whose articles were formulated or revised in 2008 or later. Revisions may be overdue in some cases.

Related parties
It should also be remembered that conflicts of interest will arise not only from the governors' other interests but from those of other related parties, notably the governors' immediate families. The register of interests should therefore include any relevant interests of these people too.

Since December 2010, the school's auditors will take an increased interest in the identities of the related parties. Emerging best practice is for the audited body to maintain a record of the names of *all* related parties and their relevant interests and to share this information with the auditors.

c) Critical incident planning

Peter Goddard

Disasters affecting schools can, in theory, come in all shapes and forms. They include the death of a pupil or member of staff from natural causes; a traffic accident involving staff or pupils during a routine day or a school journey; a deliberate act of violence against staff or pupils; a fire or major incident in a laboratory or workshop; a serious sporting accident; even a bomb incident.

Such disasters are mercifully rare. However, no school can guarantee that it will be immune from facing one, however seriously it takes health and safety; however carefully its trips policy is drawn up; however thoroughly its local authority (LA) guidelines may have been studied; however well trained its staff may be. Expanding mental horizons;

visiting new places; testing physical and mental limits via expeditions are valuable parts of growing up, but they bring associated risks. These can be assessed and reduced, but they cannot be eliminated altogether.

Moreover when things go wrong, they place sudden and forbidding burdens on a school and its staff. They have to cope with feelings of grief, guilt and insecurity amongst all involved. These demands have been accentuated by 24-hour TV news (and the appetite for stories of 'human interest'). Even apparently friendly media may interfere with communications and distract people from coping with the emergency. Schools also need to consider the impact of mobile phones: a blessing in an emergency, but sometimes a complication if schools are constantly playing catch-up with parents and pupils who have been in communication with each other from the moment the crisis broke.

For all these reasons, an increasing number of forward-thinking schools now have a comprehensive critical incident plan. Most are very willing to share their experience with others, usually at Head or bursar level – so the role of governors is to satisfy themselves that such a plan exists; that it is regularly reviewed and updated (including contact details for the key personnel), and that governors have a copy of it. This last provision is important; some emergencies take place deep into the school holidays when key personnel are dispersed and far from the school. In such an event, an informed governor can be a godsend, but someone acting in ignorance or independently of the plan and its team is all too likely to do more harm than good.

Principles and practice of good planning

No plan can cover every eventuality – but its aims are threefold:

- to prepare governors, staff and pupils for any disasters that may occur;
- to ensure that there is a plan that can be implemented swiftly in the case of an emergency caused by a disaster;
- to be a guide to actions in circumstances that are liable to strain the capacity of those handling the situation to think clearly.

In this way it can also minimize the reputational risk to the school in the longer-term.

Above all, it is essential that everybody knows:

- the roles to be performed by each person;
- the communications strategy;
- the basic principles to be followed with pupils and parents.

In summary, the plan should aim to achieve a situation in which the priority of staff at the incident is to look after pupils and each other. Dealing with the media, with parents and all other issues becomes the job of a designated disaster management team back at the school – this team will preferably be away from *immediate* accessibility to worried parents, and will be operating with a dedicated phone system. This team might, in some circumstances, include the Chairman and/or other governors.

The plan should include such matters as:

- Where a list of all those involved in the trip, and the contact numbers of their parents *etc*, has been lodged within the school *before* the trip leaves. This may be the only starting point for identifying pupils and the leader might be incapacitated or dead.

- How to ensure that the trip leader and all staff on the trip have a list of participants at all times; knowledge of how an alarm is to be raised; and a number to contact to report any disaster. This will not be the school number in case the media jam the phone lines.

- Making sure that there is a specific SMT member as a point of contact for staff in charge of each trip or visit. S/he needs to be in a position to receive all relevant information to key constituencies, including the media, as the crisis starts to break.

- How this person and/or whoever is in charge on the school site (*eg* in the holidays) can quickly contact as many members of the SMT as possible. They should have left details of their likely whereabouts prior to going away.

- Who will take on the key roles and responsibilities? These include the communications network; support for key groups; liaison with legal, insurance, foreign embassy and other relevant authorities.

- The importance of one key individual overseeing all communication with the media, and the key messages; whether or not to allow them on to the site.

- The need to contact the police immediately to ask for help in controlling access to the school.

- Detailed guidelines for communicating with all other key constituencies: who does it, and the key messages; what to put on the website; what to tell other pupils, and whether to do so in assemblies or smaller groups.

- How to reunite children with parents as quickly as possible; whether it may be helpful for parents to view the accident site so that they can share the situation with their children; whether a team member should travel to the disaster scene to take charge from the staff involved.

- The need to contact the LA to ask what resources they can make available.

- The importance of nothing being said by *anyone* that risks increasing grief, raising unnecessary anxiety or wrong-footing the school later in possible legal action.

Generally the school will be saying over and over again 'that the school will turn its attention to causes and lessons to be learned when we have done what we can do for pupils and parents'.

It may be sensible to consider some form of media and interview training for the Head and other key personnel (something that will be useful anyway), and to ensure that the school is always aware of where it could obtain counselling for post-trauma stress and grief.

When the immediate crisis has passed, it may also fall to the governors to conduct and enquiry into its circumstances, or at least to ensure that all possible lessons have been learned for the future.

Chapter 5

Public benefit
and charity legislation

Matthew Burgess

Introduction

On 14 October 2011 the Upper Tribunal published its judgment in
the Independent Schools Council's judicial review of the Charity
Commission's public benefit guidance.[1] The ruling, which runs to more
than 100 pages, has been described as the most significant development
in charity law for the last half century. For charitable schools, it represents
the end of a long period of uncertainty about the legality and effect of the
Commission's approach to the sector, and provides a workable framework
within which governors can take decisions about public benefit.[2] ISC
warmly welcomed the ruling. This chapter explains why.

The Charities Act 2006 and the legal framework

It has been said many times that the legal meaning of charity is quite
separate from the popular understanding. Indeed, this discrepancy can
be said to lie at the heart of the sector's difficulties over the years in
persuading policy makers, who are generally very alive to public opinion,
about the genuine charitable character of independent schools. The
disagreement about the meaning of 'public benefit', and what schools
must do to demonstrate it, is merely a manifestation of this confusion.

There have been many reviews of English charity law over the last 20
years, with the most significant emanating from the Prime Minister's
Strategy Unit in 2002, entitled *Public Action, Private Benefit*. It is in
this report that the Charities Act 2006 has its origins.[3] The Act is notable
in that, for the first time, it sets out statutory definitions of some basic
terminology. For example, it defines 'charity' to mean an institution that

is established for charitable purposes only. It is immediately apparent that the legal definition of charity is focused on an organisation and its purposes, and not 'charity' as a concept or value as described, perhaps most famously, in 1 Corinthians XIII.

Notably, and probably wisely, the Act refrains from defining 'public benefit'. The phrase is core to an understanding of what is, and is not, a charitable purpose, given the clear legislative statement that 'a charitable purpose is a purpose which is for the public benefit'. Rather than proffering a statutory definition of public benefit, the Act deals with its meaning in three ways. First, it expressly states that the pre-existing meaning is to be preserved. In other words, the Act acknowledges that public benefit already has a meaning under charity law, and does not seek to change it. Secondly, it states that it should not be presumed that a purpose of a particular description is for the public benefit. At the time, this was referred to as the reversal of a presumption of public benefit. Finally, the Act mandates the Commission to issue guidance to promote awareness and understanding of public benefit.

All of these issues were to be at the heart of ISC's judicial review: the pre-2006 meaning of public benefit; the effect of the reversal of the presumption of public benefit; and the degree to which the Commission crossed the line between promoting understanding and imposing a particular view of the law.

The Commission's guidance on public benefit

The Commission approached the task of issuing guidance to promote awareness and understanding of the operation of the public benefit requirement in two phases. In 2007 it published for consultation draft general guidance on public benefit: this was to become *Charities and Public Benefit: The Charity Commission's general guidance on public benefit*. In 2008 it published a series of sub-sector guidance documents, again after public consultation. Key amongst these for schools was *Public Benefit and fee-charging* and *The advancement of education for the public benefit*.

All guidance documents were framed around a set of principles that, according to the Commission, were legal requirements drawn from the underlying case law and interpreted by the Commission in the light of modern social and economic conditions. Whilst some principles were uncontroversial, focus quickly settled on principles 2b and 2c, which were in the following terms:

2b – Where benefit is to a section of the public, the opportunity to benefit must not be unreasonably restricted:
  • by geographical or other restrictions; or
  • by ability to pay any fees charged
2c – People in poverty must not be excluded from the opportunity to benefit.

The guidance – which has the status of statutory guidance, meaning that charity trustees are obliged to have regard to it – elaborated at length on these two principles. Moreover the Commission stated that the two principles overlapped to create what can perhaps be regarded as a third, free-standing, principle: that 'there must be sufficient opportunity to benefit in a material way that is related to the charity's aims for people who cannot afford the fees, including people in poverty'.

ISC was one of many bodies that responded to the Commission's consultations expressing concerns that the Commission had, in certain fundamental respects, misstated the law. For example, the Act is completely clear that 'public benefit' relates to an organisation's purposes – 'a charitable purpose is a purpose which is for the public benefit'. Why, then, did the Commission appear to look beyond an organisation's purposes (what it was established to do) to its activities (what it does and how it does it) with a view to determining whether the public benefit requirement was satisfied?

Equally, the consequences of a school failing to measure up to the Commission's guidance was opaque. Would it affect the school's charitable status; indeed, could it put the school out of business by crystallising a tax charge on its business activities or stripping its assets? The Chair of the Commission, Dame Suzi Leather, was quoted warning that 'the threshold to qualify schools for charitable status would be raised every year to ensure that they provide the maximum possible public benefit', indicating clearly that charitable status, and survival, was indeed at stake. ISC was convinced that this was wrong.

The question of poverty and affordability was also controversial. Where an organisation is established to advance education – a purpose that is uncontroversially potentially charitable – does the fact that it must levy fees to fund its activities necessarily mean that it excludes those who cannot afford those fees in a manner incompatible with its charitable nature? Or is it sufficient that its pupils form a sufficiently numerous and unrelated section of the public to meet the public benefit requirement?

The Commission's assessments of independent schools

Before the *Public Benefit and fee-charging* guidance had even been finalised, however, the Commission had already moved on to the next stage of an apparent campaign against independent schools. It announced that it would review 12 charities for compliance with its public benefit guidance. Five of these charities were ISC schools. Between October 2008 and July 2009, the Commission carried out extensive research and analysis on all 12 charities before publishing its conclusions on each charity, together with an overarching analysis entitled *Emerging Findings*.

The assessment process and the findings in relation to all five schools confirmed ISC's unease about the Commission's guidance and its approach. These centred on three aspects. First that the Commission's guidance documents, and in particular principles 2b and 2c, were wrong; secondly that the Commission's apparent focus on what schools were doing, which the assessment process underscored, missed the point of public benefit being a purposes test, not an activities test. And thirdly, that even if the guidance was right and an examination of activities appropriate, the Commission had gone far beyond its regulatory role of promoting an understanding of public benefit and was, in effect, substituting its own judgements on the type and amount of activities required for a school to continue as a charity.

There was a particular concern about an apparent hierarchy of activities or benefits that the Commission considered valuable in the context of a public benefit assessment. The key concern was the weight given to bursaries. Bursaries, and in particular full or 100% bursaries, appeared to be the cornerstone of the Commission's approach to public benefit. Of the five assessed schools, only one received an unqualified report on the basis of its bursary provision. Two schools received qualified assessments, in each case with reservations expressed about the relatively few full bursaries available. And two schools received adverse findings, with the level of bursary provision being highlighted as the key failing. So, despite protestations to the contrary from the Commission, the sector had a strong steer that bursary provision, with a weighting towards full bursaries, was the hallmark of public benefit.

The focus on bursaries – and indeed on the right kind of bursaries – led to many other consequences. Limited resources channelled into means-tested bursaries threatened the viability of other, equally valid, programmes: hardship awards for pupils whose parents have fallen on hard times; scholarships and awards for children with music, sporting or academic talents; partnerships with local schools; community outreach programmes; partnerships with schools in lesser-developed economies overseas. At the same time, schools were beginning to look at whether fee increases for all might be required to fund bursary places for the few. These were all examples of decisions that, the sector felt, should properly be taken by and within schools looking at their own particular circumstances, ethos and approach to education, rather than being driven by the external consideration of anticipating a Commission public benefit assessment.

The Commission's approach to partnership activity by schools was particularly revealing of the gulf between its stated approach in its guidance and its actual determinations on the ground. As can be read in the Commission's assessment reports, all five schools demonstrated significant partnership activities, with Manchester Grammar School, for example, recording a hugely impressive range of activities involving its pupils and staff, local children, local community and overseas schools. And yet the Commission dismissed them all, in one line applying to all 12 charities: 'in none of the assessments were [non-bursary benefits] significant enough on their own' to meet the Commission's understanding of the public benefit requirement.

The ISC challenge and the Attorney General's reference

The approach indicated by the assessment reports made a legal confrontation with the Commission almost inevitable, and ISC formally launched its application for judicial review in February 2010. Less predictable, perhaps, was the involvement of the Attorney General who announced in July 2010 that he too was concerned about legal uncertainties surrounding the meaning of public benefit and intended to refer them to the Charity Tribunal for clarification.

When the hearing finally opened in May 2011, therefore, it was formally two separate proceedings: an application by ISC for judicial review of the Commission's guidance, and a reference by the Attorney General of specific questions for consideration and response by the Tribunal. In essence, though, the issues were the same: were principles 2b and 2c, and the separate free standing principle regarding the sufficiency of opportunity to benefit, correct expressions of the law of public benefit? If they were, could more clarity be given about where the line was to be drawn in particular cases? And if they were not, what did the law truly require?

The Upper Tribunal's findings

In relation to the Commission's guidance, the Tribunal's findings are unequivocal:

> ... we conclude that principle 2b of the principles of public benefit on which the Guidance focuses is wrong. As the Charity Commission states in Fee-Charging, that principle and principle 2c overlap and we conclude that principle 2c, at least as explained in the Guidance, is also wrong. It follows that, as explained above, various passages in Public Benefit and Fee Charging which are based on those principles are themselves obscure or wrong in a number of respects. The Advancement of Education for the Public Benefit will also be affected by what we have said about the principles, although principles 2b and 2c are not themselves discussed there. It follows from those conclusions that the Guidance should be corrected. [The Commission's QC] did submit to us that if we came to the conclusion that the Guidance was indeed wrong, we should

nevertheless conclude that the Charity Commission had taken a reasonable view of the law in framing it as they did and should refrain from quashing any part of it, leaving it to the Commission to amend or withdraw the Guidance as they saw fit to reflect this Decision. Although we have every sympathy with the Commission in the difficulty of the task it faced in producing guidance on this area of law, we do not think it right that we should simply leave matters to the Charity Commission to correct without granting the ISC any relief at all.[4]

Equally importantly, the Tribunal draws a very clear distinction between the charitable status of a school, on the one hand, and the proper exercise by the governors of their duties as charity trustees on the other:

The status of an existing registered charity and the duties of the trustees have not been changed by the 2006 Act. As to status, either it was entitled to be registered before the 2006 Act or it was not. If it was, its purposes must have been for the public benefit as that term was then understood and, since we are dealing with schools where there is no presumption made under the pre-2006 Act law for the reasons we have given, it thus fulfils the public benefit test under the 2006 Act. Accordingly, whether such a school is a charity within the meaning of the 2006 Act does not now turn on the way in which it operates any more than it did before. Its status as a charity depends on what it was established to do, not on what it does.

So, for schools already registered as charities, their charitable status is not at issue. Failure to meet a continuing public benefit test becomes a question of governor liability. One can perhaps draw an analogy with companies registered at Companies House: actions by the directors that are in breach of duty do not affect the company's legal status. Indeed, the responsibility placed on the governors to ensure that the school continues to operate in line with its purposes for the public benefit is no different to the raft of other responsibilities assumed by governors, such as ensuring compliance with independent school standards, meeting health and safety requirements, and safeguarding children.

What is the content of those public benefit duties for governors? First, the Tribunal decides as a matter of principle that the impact of fees is a relevant consideration:

> A trust which excludes the poor from benefit cannot be a charity. There is no case which decides that point, but we consider it is right as a matter of principle, given the underlying concept of charity from early times.'

The Tribunal agrees that it is highly unlikely that any school does, as a matter of its constitution, exclude the poor.[5] It also acknowledges the financial pressures on schools that inevitably drive what schools can do for those who are not fully contributing to the running costs of the school:

> Schools cannot as easily admit one person as another. Who a school is able to admit depends on the financial state of the school, the size of its endowment and the way in which those running the school choose to prioritise expenditure (*eg* on providing scholarships or keeping class sizes down by employing more staff) and the facilities which it provides. It is necessary for all of the schools to charge fees. They do not, it seems to us, choose the majority of their students because of a preference for students who have as a characteristic an ability to pay fees; they do so because they cannot afford not to choose such students. And, of course, the charging of fees does not, as we have seen, *per se* preclude charitable status.

Nevertheless, the Tribunal rules that where a school makes no provision for the poor – or, to be more precise, makes provision that is only minimal or token – its governors have not discharged their duties. But what the governors do, and how they do it, is for them and them alone to decide. In particular, it is not for the Commission to substitute its own assessment of what is a 'reasonable' level of provision. In fact, the test is not one of reasonableness at all:

> Although it is necessary that there must be more than a *de minimis* or token benefit for the poor, once that low threshold is reached, what the trustees decide to do in the running of the school is a matter for them,

subject to acting within the range within which trustees can properly act. That is something entirely different from imposing on the trustees the view of anyone else about what is 'reasonable'.

This is all a matter of judgment for the trustees. There will be no one right answer. There will be one or more minimum benefits below which no reasonable trustees would go but subject to that, the level of provision and the method of its provision is properly a matter for them and not for the Charity Commission or the court. We deliberately avoid using the word 'reasonable' ... It is not for the Charity Commission or the Tribunal or the court to impose on trustees of a school their own idea of what is, and what is not, reasonable. The courts have never done that in the context of their supervision of trustees of private trusts and the same should apply to charities. There is nothing in the 2006 Act (including the duty to issue the Guidance) which changes that position. But trustees are under the ultimate control of the courts. There is always a range of actions which they can take in a given situation. There is, of course, a limit outside which they must not step. But the identification of that limit is not based on a test of reasonableness.

The Chair of the Commission has already commented on this finding in the following terms, and provides a useful indication of how the Commission might approach rewritten guidance: 'What the Tribunal does not think is correct is that the wording of our guidance seems to imply that trustees have to provide a reasonable amount of benefit for people who cannot afford the fees.'

Finally, in considering what might be done to make provision for the poor, the apparent weighting of means-tested full bursaries over everything else has also been disapproved:

When it comes to considering whether a school which is a charity is operating for the public benefit in accordance with its charitable purposes, the primary focus must be on the direct benefits which it provides. Scholarships or other forms of direct assistance to students are therefore important. Account can certainly be taken of other direct benefits such as [arrangements under which students from local state schools can attend classes in subjects not otherwise readily available to them] and [sharing of teachers or teaching facilities with local state schools]. Account can be taken of [making available (whether on the internet or otherwise) teaching materials used in the school] since they are clearly available to the whole community ... we consider that [making available to students of local state schools other facilities such as playing fields, sports halls, swimming pools or sports grounds] are to be taken into account in deciding whether a school which is a charity is operating for the public benefit.

Indeed, benefits that the Commission had rejected as being too tangential to be relevant may also be taken into account, although they will rarely be determinative:

Once provision is made for the 'poor', which is more than *de minimis* or merely token, we see no reason why an identified wider benefit should not be taken into account in deciding whether, overall, the way in which the school is being operated is for the public benefit.

Conclusion

Schools and governors will be faced with plenty of advice about what the ruling really means, and how it is to be interpreted. Many law firms and accountants have rushed into print already. The Commission will withdraw its fee-charging guidance and parts of the general guidance to reissue them in substance, it is to be hoped, closer to the law than its previous attempts.[6] ISC will also issue full guidance to schools on the practical implications of the judgment.

This chapter is not intended to replace or foreshadow all that guidance. Instead, let us draw one simple proposition from the judgment: on decisions affecting what a school does to live up to its charitable purposes, it is the governors who are in the driving seat. No school can operate solely for the benefit of its full fee-paying pupils; but no 21st century independent school does. It is for the governors to decide what the school can do, and how it can do it. Governors should approach this task in the right spirit, asking themselves the right questions: what is the charity established to do, who does it seek to benefit, how can it meet its objects whilst living within its means and maintaining a viable future? A governing board that takes this approach will, almost by definition, arrive at answers falling within the range of rational, unchallengeable, decisions.

Making good public benefit decisions is, in truth, simply an exercise of good corporate governance. A board that follows due process, considers the right issues and acts rationally has nothing to fear.

References

1. The Independent Schools Council -v- The Charity Commission and others [2011] UKUT 421 (TCC). The final order was issued on 8 December 2011.
2. I refer to governors in this chapter on the assumption that the governors are the trustees of the charity in question, although this is not always the case.
3. I refer to the Charities Act 2006 in the present tense as this is, at the time of writing, still fully in force. There is a Charities Bill currently under consideration that is intended to replace the 2006 Act and consolidate it with other charities legislation. And a review of certain provisions of the 2006 Act, including the operation of the public benefit requirement, is also getting underway.
4. On 2 December 2011 the Tribunal granted relief by giving the Commission 21 days to withdraw the disputed parts of the guidance, including the fee charging guidance in entirety, failing which the Tribunal will quash them.
5. In fact, this was not in dispute in the proceedings. ISC agreed that an organisation established 'to educate the rich', for example, would not have purposes for the public benefit.
6. At time of writing it is anticipated that the guidance will now be withdrawn; see reference 4.

Chapter 6

Child protection requirements

Jonathan Cook

'Governing bodies are … accountable for ensuring their establishment
has effective child protection policies and procedures in place…'
(A guide to the law for school governors, published by the DfE)

Introduction

Governors will recognise that they have a multi-faceted duty of care
towards all in their school community. Most will be, or will soon become,
familiar with the demands of Health & Safety legislation, but when it
comes to Safeguarding and Child Protection, they can be forgiven for
being confused as to exactly what is required of them. They know they
have to do something, but often struggle to identify exactly what this
might be.

This may, in part, be a result of the huge amount of guidance now made
available to schools. As noted in Volume 7 of this series, *The Work of the
Bursar*, the full extent to which the whole process has mushroomed was
highlighted in Professor Munro's first report:

> Professionals working with children and young people in social care,
> health, education, and police services have access to detailed guidance
> and procedures to inform the way they work together to safeguard
> children and young people from harm. Parton (Parton, N (2010), *The
> Increasing Complexity of 'Working Together to Safeguard Children in
> England'*) reports that the first formulation of government guidance
> in 1974 was seven pages long, whilst the latest statutory guidance,
> published in 2010, has 390 pages and makes references to ten other
> pieces of supplementary guidance that provide a further 424 pages.

The confusion may also be partly due to whole raft of pseudo 'best practice' activity that has emerged as schools seek to 'do the right thing'. Here one thinks of schools that have spent a considerable amount of money, time and effort in renewing Criminal Record Bureau (CRB) disclosures every three years. Yet just a small amount of research on the Department for Education (DfE) website would have revealed that this is not required.

It is against this backdrop of mushrooming legislation and contradictory advice that this chapter is written. Its purpose is to:

- Briefly review the exponential growth in legislation and guidance over the past 25 years, in order to understand how complicated a subject this has become.
- Clarify some of the terms used when thinking about child protection, and where this responsibility fits within the larger issue of safeguarding children from harm.
- Set out for governors their responsibilities for child protection within their schools.

A brief history

Sadly, the problem of child abuse is not new. Over many years – in an unknown number of schools of all types: day as well as boarding; maintained as well as independent; senior as well as junior – a small proportion of staff mistreated children. The first significant Act of Parliament for the Prevention of Cruelty to Children was passed as long ago as 1889, and there was periodic new legislation throughout the 20th century. However, until a few decades ago it tended to centre on problems within families, or in connection with children in foster care, or those living under the supervision of social services.

By contrast, from the end of the 1980s, the speed of change dramatically increased – particularly with regard to schools. The impetus to ensure that all children should be protected from harm stemmed in part from the investigation by Esther Rantzen and her BBC TV *That's Life* team into the appalling state of affairs at Crookham Court boarding school (1991), which led to major new requirements on educational establishments – for example, to provide private 24-hour phoning-out facilities for boarders. And it was from the *That's Life* involvement that *Childline* was born.

Meanwhile the past 30 years have seen a continuing cycle of tragedy within households, as children continue to be abused and die; inquiries then take place into what went wrong; followed by copious recommendations to put things right, leading to legislation and statutory guidance to try to ensure that proper practices and procedures are in place to protect children.

Sadly, this cycle of activity has been remarkably unsuccessful. Take just two tragedies, separated by 31 years: Maria Colwell, aged eight, died from abuse in January 1973 and Ryan Lovell-Hancox, aged three, in December 2008. The common feature in the lessons learned from reports on these two cases is that there were numerous agencies involved with both these children prior to their deaths – no fewer than 14 in the latter case – and yet there was a breakdown in communications between them. Simplistically, agencies failed to talk with each other. And yet, in the 31 years between these two cases, there has been a raft of advice issued to try to avoid exactly this happening.

Just to drive home the point about 'copious recommendations': in 2009, Lord Laming wrote one report on Child Protection for the DfE, and Sir Roger Singleton two. Within these three reports there were exactly 100 recommendations to improve child protection; these were all accepted by the government: some were implemented instantly; some required legislative changes; and all necessitated amendments to guidance – and this all takes time. It is thus unsurprising that schools are often left wondering as to exactly what is required.

Legislation and guidance

The key milestones along the child protection path, which those involved with child protection may often come across, are as follows:

1989: The Children Act. This Act stated the basic legal principle in all public and private proceedings concerning children that the welfare of the child was paramount; enshrined the principle that delay was inimical to a child's welfare; created the role of independent visitor, a voluntary post, to befriend and assist children and young people in care, and made clear a statutory obligation on all professionals to report suspected child abuse.

1999: *Working Together to Safeguard Children*. This presented a national framework for child protection practice for everyone working with children and families.

1999: The Protection of Children Act. This enabled the CRB to disclose information about people who were included on the Protection of Children Act (PoCA) List, or List 99, along with criminal records. The Act provided for a 'one-stop' shop system for checking people seeking to work with children.

2003: The Laming Report, following the death of Victoria Climbie, found that health, police and social services had missed 12 opportunities to save her. This report lead to the publication of a Green Paper called *Every Child Matters*.

2004: This implemented the recommendations of *Every Child Matters* through another Children Act. Its main aims were for every child, whatever their background or circumstances, to have the support they need to:

- be healthy;
- stay safe;
- enjoy and achieve;
- make a positive contribution;
- achieve economic wellbeing.

2004: The Bichard Inquiry report, following the deaths of two 10-year-old girls in Soham at the hands of their school caretaker Ian Huntley, was published. The inquiry report made 31 recommendations. One was to implement a registration scheme for people working with children and vulnerable adults such as the elderly. The development of this recommendation led to the foundation of the Independent Safeguarding Authority (ISA).

2006: The Safeguarding Vulnerable Groups Act 2006 picked up on one of the recommendations of the Bichard Inquiry. It established the legal basis for the ISA to manage the two lists of people barred from working with children and/or vulnerable adults. It replaced the previous barred lists, List 99, the PoCA list, the scheme relating to the Protection of Vulnerable Adults (PoVA) and Disqualification Orders. The Act also placed a statutory duty on all those working with vulnerable groups to register and undergo an advanced vetting process with criminal sanctions for non-compliance.

2006: The statutory guidance *Working Together to Safeguard Children* was updated. It continued to set out the ways in which organisations and individuals should work together to safeguard and promote the wellbeing of children. It also created the role of Local Authority Designated Officer, 'LADO', responsible for managing allegations of abuse against adults who work with children.

2007: *Safeguarding Children and Safer Recruitment in Education* was published. This has been the key document for schools over the past few years and is still extant, although likely to be replaced during the lifetime of the coalition government. It sets out recruitment best practice (some underpinned by legislation) for schools, and also details the process for dealing with allegations of abuse against staff.

2009: In March, the Laming Report entitled *The Protection of Children in England: A Progress Report*, reported on the progress being made across the country to implement effective arrangements for safeguarding children. Laming made 58 recommendations centred on the proposition that child protection had become a 'Cinderella service' tied up in too much red tape

2009: In March, the Singleton Report, *Keeping our School Safe*, was published and clarified some of the issues that had emerged since the introduction of the Vetting and Barring Scheme (VBS). The central message underpinning the 32 recommendations was that the government needed to streamline the confusing and overlapping regulations and standards that made up the legal framework for child protection in independent schools. Singleton found that these arrangements caused confusion for schools, which had to make their way through a 'thicket' of regulations.

2009: In December, a second report by Sir Roger Singleton, *Drawing the line*, was published. The VBS, launched in October 2009, introduced a new safeguarding regime under the control of the ISA. This scheme received much public criticism and this report made ten recommendations.

2010: *Working Together to Safeguard Children* was updated to take into account the recommendations of Lord Laming's 2009 progress report.

2011: The Education Bill was published on 11 February 2011. At the time of writing the proposals in this legislation and in the Protection of Freedom Bill will bring about yet further changes to the child protection regime.

Definitions

The Education Act 2002, which came into force on 1 June 2004, placed a duty on governing bodies of schools to have arrangements in place to ensure that they 'exercise their functions with a view to safeguarding and promoting the welfare of children'. The DfE defines the phrase 'Safeguarding and Promoting the Welfare of Children' as:

- Protecting children from maltreatment
- Preventing impairment of children's health or development
- Ensuring that children are growing up in circumstances consistent with the provision of safe and effective care.

Safeguarding covers more than the contribution made to child protection in relation to individual children. It encompasses issues such as:

- Pupil health and safety
- Bullying
- Medical needs
- First aid
- School security
- Drugs and substance misuse.

Schools must have policies to cover all of these areas. However, the focus for this chapter is firmly on child protection – in other words, the activity that is undertaken to protect specific children who are suffering, or are likely to suffer, significant harm.

The responsibilities of school governors

Governors of independent schools are accountable for ensuring their establishment has effective policies and procedures in place and monitoring the school's compliance with them. Guidance on exactly what is required is set out in the DfE's guidance document entitled *Safeguarding Children and Safer Recruitment in Education.* (It is anticipated that this guidance will be revised in due course). A school's LA will have what is called a Local Safeguarding Children Board (LSCB) and this Board is also a valuable source of advice.

The DfE requires governors of independent schools to ensure that:

- The school has a child protection policy and procedures in place. This policy must be published on the open or public part of the school's website or, where no website exists, must be sent as hard copy to current and prospective parents on request. Schools that are charities will wish to note the Charity Commission's advice on what the Commission terms the essential inclusions for a child protection policy, namely:
  - the welfare of the child is paramount;
  - all children without exception have the right to protection from abuse regardless of gender, ethnicity, disability, sexuality or beliefs;
  - the policy is approved and endorsed by the board of trustees;
  - who the policy applies to (*ie* all trustees, staff and volunteers);
  - children and parents are informed of the policy and procedures as appropriate;
  - all concerns, and allegations of abuse will be taken seriously by trustees, staff and volunteers and responded to appropriately – this may require a referral to children's services and in emergencies, the police;
  - a commitment to safe recruitment, selection and vetting;
  - reference to principles, legislation and guidance that underpin the policy;
  - arrangements for policy and procedures review;
  - reference to all associated policies and procedures which promote children's safety and welfare *eg* with regards to: health and safety, anti-bullying, protection of children online, and photography.

- The school operates safe recruitment procedures and makes sure that all appropriate checks are carried out on staff and volunteers who work with children. Note that the CRB check for the Chairman of governors has to be carried out by the DfE and not the school.

- Any panel involved in the recruitment of staff has at least one member who has undertaken the Children's Workforce Development Council (CWDC), or equivalent, safer recruitment training.

- The school has procedures for dealing with allegations of abuse against members of staff or volunteers that comply with locally agreed inter-agency procedures. These include procedures for the governors to liaise with other agencies in the event that allegations are made involving the Head.

- A senior member of the school's management structure is designated to take lead responsibility for dealing with child protection issues and liaising with other agencies where necessary. As in maintained schools, the designated person need not be a teacher but s/he needs to have the status and authority within the school management structure to carry out the duties of the post, including committing resources to child protection matters and where appropriate directing other staff. In many independent schools a single designated person will be sufficient, but a deputy should always be available to act in the designated person's absence, and in schools that are organised into separate junior and senior parts on different sites or with a separate management line, there should be a designated person for each part or site.

- In addition to basic child protection training, the designated person undertakes training in inter-agency working that is provided by, or to standards set by, the LSCB, and refresher training at two yearly intervals to keep his/her knowledge and skills up-to-date.

- The Head, and all other staff who work with children, undertake training that equips them with the knowledge and skills necessary to carry out their responsibilities for child protection, which is kept up-to-date by refresher training at three yearly intervals, and temporary staff and volunteers who work with children are made aware of the school's arrangements for child protection and their responsibilities.

- Any deficiencies or weaknesses in regard to child protection arrangements are remedied without delay.

- The governors undertake an annual review of the school's policies and procedures relating to safeguarding, and how the above duties have been discharged.

Boarding schools

All schools that provide residential (boarding) accommodation for children are required to meet the additional welfare and safeguarding standards set out in the National Minimum Standards for Boarding. These standards have recently been revised and reduced in number.

Extended schools, before and after school activities and holiday lets

The governing body of a school controls the use of the school premises both during and outside school hours, except where a trust deed allows a person other than the governing body to control the use of the premises, or a transfer of control agreement has been made. Governing bodies can enter into transfer of control agreements in order to share control of the school premises with another body, or transfer control to it. The other body, known as the 'controlling body', will control the occupation and use of the premises during the times specified in the agreement. Transferring control of the premises to local community groups, sports associations and service providers can enable school facilities to be used without needing ongoing management or administrative time from school staff.

Where the governing body provides services or activities directly under the supervision or management of school staff, the school's arrangements for child protection will apply. Where services or activities are provided separately by another body, the governing body should seek assurance that the body concerned has appropriate policies and procedures in place in regard to safeguarding children and child protection and that there are arrangements to liaise with the school on these matters where appropriate.

Conclusion

As with some of the other chapters in this book the details can look very daunting – especially to those new to school governing. It is comforting to know, however, that a vast amount of training and back-up advice is now available to a school's management from LA and other agencies, both in terms of the policies to be drawn up and their day-to-day application when difficult cases arise, and the prominence accorded to child protection within the inspection system (see chapter 7) should ensure that no school can ignore current requirements – however rapidly the detailed requirements may change.

Great advances have been made in recent decades in the protection of children. It is, for example, markedly harder than it once was for staff known to be suspect to be quietly passed on from one school to another. Yet no system is foolproof and we should never be complacent. No school is more at risk in reputation terms than one that adopts a cavalier attitude to child protection, especially if it is caught out by parents or inspectors and then subsequently tries to cover things up. Child protection is, and will remain, a topic of great concern to the public at large – and consequently to the media and politicians.

Even more importantly though, we *all* have a moral duty to do all we can to protect children of all ages. Governors will wish to focus extremely closely on it to ensure those in their care are protected from harm. The pace of legislative change in this area has slowed, and it is to be hoped that the Freedom Bill and Education Bill going through Parliament in 2011-12 will clarify and stabilize things; there must always be close vigilance in this area. As Lord Bichard noted in 2004: 'The harsh reality is that if a sufficiently devious person is determined to seek out opportunities to work their evil, no one can guarantee that they will be stopped.'

It is the role of both governors and management to ensure that a school does all it can to thwart them.

Chapter 7

Governance and the inspection system

Joy Richardson

"The inspectors are on their way – next week." The phone call to the school, perhaps anticipated but impossible to predict, sets in train a flurry of activity shot through with varying degrees of anxiety. Short notice inspections, now the norm, are predicated on the notion of 'inspection readiness' to which all schools should aspire. The chairman of governors will be quick to hear that inspectors are coming, but the whole governing body has a responsibility for ensuring that state of readiness.

The governing body is ultimately accountable for the quality of education provided by the school, and for ensuring compliance with legal requirements. But in inspection, the governing body is also accounted *to*, in receiving an objective analysis of the school's performance. Governors have a responsibility for protecting the school's reputation, and will have a keen eye on how the published report will be read by fee payers, current or prospective. Inspection can also be used positively to add to the governing body's understanding of the school and the clarity of its vision for the future. In particular, the examination of governance within the inspection framework should help to focus minds on the effectiveness of the governing body itself.

Who inspects?
The Office for Standards in Education (Ofsted) was founded in 1992, to extend the work of Her Majesty's Inspectors (HMI) into a unified system of inspection for every state school. HMI continued to visit independent schools, while the independent school associations began to formulate their own approaches to inspection in order to guarantee the

quality of member schools. This led in 2002 to the establishment of the Independent Schools Inspectorate (ISI) with responsibility, approved by law, for the inspection of schools in membership of the associations of the Independent Schools Council (ISC).

ISI has several masters. It reports to the Department for Education (DfE) on schools' compliance with the Independent Schools Standards Regulations. Schools must be registered with the DfE, and this compliance is a condition of their registration. Ofsted, on behalf of the DfE, monitors the quality of ISI inspections. Until 2009, Ofsted directly inspected the Early Years Foundation Stage (EYFS: the provision to the age of five) in independent schools. This has now been handed over to ISI, allowing a more rational and streamlined approach to inspection. The process has continued with the inspection of boarding, previously separately inspected and reported on by Ofsted, now also coming under ISI's remit.

ISI is an independent body, but it consults with the ISC associations and the schools that they represent, who pay for inspection through an annual levy. Within the legal constraints of its constitution, it is able to develop its own distinctive approach to inspection, reflecting the nature of the schools it inspects. Central to its approach is a commitment to 'peer review'. Inspections are led by reporting inspectors who are professionally experienced in inspection and, in many cases, have been Heads in independent schools. Team inspectors, usually Heads, deputies or senior staff currently working in comparable schools, support them. This has a two-way value. Inspectors bring up-to-date knowledge and expectation, and return to their own school with a wider perspective as well as skills gained through inspecting. It is a valued form of training that governors do well to encourage.

Inspection readiness

The school's own declared aims provide a benchmark for evaluating how well it is doing, and this allows ISI inspections to take account, in some measure, of the distinctive characteristics of each school. These aims are summarised in the introduction to the report and judgements in each section refer back to them. Statements of aims may often appear anodyne and universal in application, but governors should know what they are, assist in sharpening them and challenge the school about relating vision to practice.

Schools are asked to complete an annual return for ISI, providing information that is drawn on before an inspection. Schools are also invited to complete, as part of the pre-inspection information they provide, a self-evaluation form (SEF), part of which is the school's assessment of the quality of its governance. This details, under each aspect covered on inspection, the school's own judgement of how well it is doing; an analysis of strengths and areas for action, and any particular points on which the school would like feedback from the inspection. The school has full access to the inspection guidelines and makes its judgements against the same criteria that inspectors will be using. This is particularly important for the school when checking its own compliance with regulatory requirements in advance of the inspection.

Self evaluation has been long embedded in the maintained sector and has led to shorter inspections, at shorter notice, that test the robustness of the school's own evaluation rather than starting from scratch. Completion of the SEF was voluntary in ISI inspections but, as almost all schools chose to complete it, it became an integral part of the package of information required from schools before an inspection. Now, insistence on completion of the SEF by state schools has been watered down, in order to ease the bureaucratic burden, and it is once again optional for ISI inspections. However, inspection will continue to explore how the school evaluates itself, reflecting an intention that inspection should be 'done with' rather than 'done to' the school.

Governors should be aware of the school's self-evaluation process, which, at best, develops a shared view of what is going well and what could be better, and feeds into the school's development planning. In many cases they may be directly involved, for example in making an evaluation about the effectiveness of governance. Any governors who meet with inspectors during the inspection need to be fully conversant with what the school has submitted.

Inspectors refer back to the previous inspection report and comment on any significant changes since that time, or progress in response to recommendations. Governors should be reminded of what was said last time (the report remains on the ISI website until replaced by a new one), and should be updated on any actions that have followed.

Dealing with regulatory requirements

The last decade has seen exponential growth in the regulatory requirements imposed on independent schools. The responsibility of governing bodies for ensuring compliance has grown in equal measure. This has burst into the consciousness of governors as the inspection regime has taken on the task of policing compliance.

The Independent School Standards Regulations (ISSRs) for England were introduced with statutory force in 2002 and have been serially amended and added to since. The same standards apply to all independent schools in England, whether or not they are inspected by ISI. Ofsted inspects those independent schools outside the ISC umbrella (more than 1000). In other parts of the UK, their own national inspectorate is responsible for the inspection of independent schools and each country has its own formulation of the regulatory requirements. There is no escape.

The standards, with their multiple sub sections and cross-references, have run to a checklist of several hundred items. The separate, but overlapping, National Minimum Standards for boarding schools more than doubled the total item count. The EYFS requirements, again overlapping but formulated separately from the ISSRs, added another hundred or so. The need for radical regulatory pruning, and re-writing in sensible English, has been widely recognised and governors have been making their voice heard on this. The roll back is underway. The boarding regulations have been vigorously pruned and the EYFS requirements are under review. In other areas, regulatory adjustments are being made but the process will take some time to complete.

In the meantime, governors must make sure that they fulfil their responsibility to ensure the school's compliance with legal requirements. Compliance with these standards is a condition of the school's registration with the DfE. Non-compliance can trigger follow-up action instigated by the DfE through ISI and, *in extremis*, school closure. This has concentrated the mind, although fears of 'failure' on minor points have often been overblown.

The ISI Handbook provides specific and detailed guidance about the standards and what is required to meet them. This is not recommended as bedtime reading for governors (except as a cure for insomnia), but they should know who has read it, the mechanisms used for ensuring compliance, and who has signed off the checklist before an inspection.

Governors have a duty to review the school's policies and their effectiveness and must decide how to do this most efficiently. Child protection, or safeguarding, comes at the top of the list. The governing body is required to undertake an annual review of the school's policy and procedures and how well these have worked. Other policies closely scrutinised by inspectors to ensure that they meet requirements include those for first aid, anti-bullying, health and safety and dealing with complaints.

The regulations that have perhaps caused greatest anxiety for schools are the complex requirements concerning the making and recording of safeguarding checks on staff and others connected with the school, including governors themselves. Governors must be satisfied that all checks are carried out as required, and that the school has a watertight system for recording these checks. Problems are most likely to arise when responsibility is too dispersed or falls between the academic and bursarial sides of the operation.

The cycle of inspection that began in 2009 was designed to provide a necessary focus on regulations while supporting schools in becoming fully compliant. Schools, and governors, learn quickly and the level of non-compliance dropped rapidly over the course of the inspection cycle. The new integrated inspection framework, from 2012, provides for a single inspection event over four days with a regulatory emphasis on day one, followed by three days with a strong focus on teaching and learning. Inspection follows a six-year cycle, with a short intervening inspection of EYFS and boarding every three years. Schools continue to be inspected at five days' notice.

Inspecting the quality of governance

The inspection of governance forms part of the inspection framework. The quality of governance is judged against published inspection criteria and it is important for governors to be briefed on these. Inspectors meet with the Chairman of governors and, if appropriate, others carrying a particular area of responsibility. It is not usual to meet the whole governing body. Discussion focuses broadly on the questions:

- How well does the governing body know the school?
- Do governance arrangements ensure effective oversight?
- Are legal responsibilities fully discharged?

Even in privately owned schools with no formal governing body, inspection explores how well the functions of governance are carried out. Where there is an overarching trust or foundation, information will be sought from the central body as well as at local level about the operation of governance.

Governors are expected to be aware of the school's strategic vision, its key strengths in relation to its aims, and areas for improvement identified in its development planning. The purpose is not to extract admissions of weakness, but to evaluate the insight, support and challenge provided by governors.

As with other aspects of inspection, the final concern is with outcomes, not with a particular way of doing things. There is no 'right' committee structure, but no part of the school's work should fall below the governors' radar. Inspection is likely to find shortcomings in governance where there is an imbalance of attention to different areas of the school's work. What is the balance of discussion between finance and buildings on the one hand and education on the other? Are governors as well informed about the junior or pre-prep school as about the senior school?

A governing body that regularly evaluates its own effectiveness has a head start in inspection: it will already have asked itself the awkward questions.

The future of inspection

Inspection has evolved and is continuing to do so. ISI is embarking on a fourth framework for inspection. It is continuing to respond to DfE requirements, the changing pattern of inspection for maintained schools and the views of independent schools themselves. The length and frequency of inspection is changing, and the balance between compliance and education as the focus for inspection is shifting.

Whatever the packaging, inspection will continue to play a part in providing objective evaluation of the school's success, in terms of outcomes for pupils. Inspection reports will continue to be valued by parents as a window on the school. Inspection processes, including lesson observation and self-evaluation, are becoming rooted in schools, disturbing complacency and feeding ambition for improvement.

One inspection team arrived at a school to be greeted by a notice, quoting a foot soldier facing an army of invaders in ancient Greece:

> I have made preparation as best I can.
> I have sacrificed to the gods for my peace of mind.
> Now I stand ready with my doors open and proclaim
> 'Let them come!'

Schools, and governors, may be ambivalent about inspection, but the inspection call invariably triggers a determination to show the school at its very best. Whether through inspection or through preparation for inspection, the process is likely to leave the school a better place – or, at the very least, to unite everyone in its defence.

Chapter 8

The role of the Chairman

Stephen Dorrell

The principles of good chairmanship of a governing body are the same, whether the school is boarding or day, and whatever its nature, size, wealth and the age range of the pupils it educates. Many boards meet together formally for as little as ten hours per year. There are also likely to be a number of sub-committees as well as informal social occasions. However long the time spent, the sum total of this activity needs to produce two results: effective performance and a coherent forward strategy. These in their turn are determined through clear objectives and an effective budgeting process.

Above all, the Chairman and the members of the board must have a very clear understanding of the difference between policy and management. The board's role is to determine the direction of travel for the school (wherever possible, reflecting the advice that it receives from the Head and the senior management team). The Head's role is to persuade the board of the wisdom of what is being proposed, and to come up with an acceptable method of delivering it.

It is always tempting for governors, and especially for the Chairman, to stray into management matters, but the board's role is to appoint the Head, CEO or whatever title the person at the top of the management pyramid has, and then to support, guide, encourage, and get momentum rolling. If it fails to roll, and there are no signs of a coherent strategic plan emerging, the board may be called upon to provide some blue-sky thinking and, in strategic terms, to be willing to think the unthinkable.

It may even be necessary occasionally to prod, to pressurise or to persuade, to steer into pastures new, to negotiate an early retirement, or *in extremis* (or in crisis) to dismiss – but this is indeed a last resort. Otherwise, it is the Chairman's job simply to let the Head be leader of the pack, and to ensure that the governing body is taken along with whatever is being proposed.

Key components of good chairmanship

What, then, are the key ingredients of the Chairman's role? Essentially they boil down to these:

- Within the limits already described, the board has ultimate responsibility for the wellbeing and development of the school. The governors are the guardians of its reputation and ethos for the long term, beyond the tenure of any individual Head.

- Once aims and plan are clear, a process needs to evolve: form should follow function. It is the Chairman's job to ensure that the board runs effectively. This includes getting the board periodically to review the articles that underpin its work and its status (for example, should it be incorporated? – See chapter 4). There should be an annual review of the work of committees and of their membership.

- The Chairman must personally ensure that the board's activities and strategic direction conform to any charitable or other objects laid down in law. It is normally the Chairman who signs off the accounts and any charity return. The senior management should see to the detail and this should not be micromanaged by the board, but the Chairman must be confident that the process has been sound.

- The Chairman is the public face of the school in certain situations. These include public occasions such as Speech Day, when your role is to give an upbeat impression, and to give a brief account to parents of the board's activities, whilst leaving the Head to describe the school's recent achievements. It might include chairing meetings of parents to explain *major* changes of strategy. The board can also be an invaluable 'deflector of heat' away from the Head when changes judged necessary may be unpopular.

- It is the Chairman's responsibility to ensure an appropriate response in dealing with formal complaints, and with appeals that have already been considered by the management but where a resolution has not been reached. The school should, of course, have clear complaints and disciplinary procedures that have been checked by lawyers. The governors are in this sense a final court of appeal, so a key part of your role in this situation is to decide how and at what stage you and other key governors should be deployed. Any of you who have been at all involved in the earlier, informal attempts at conflict resolution become automatically ineligible to sit on a panel to hear a formal appeal.

Essentially, a great deal of your time and effort as Chairman is expended on oiling the wheels in various ways, albeit mostly in the background. This involves creating and sustaining harmonious and purposeful relationships between the governors and the management, and helping to foster a sense of good and open government among staff, parents and (in an age when senior pupils have increasingly strident opinions) members of the school. You create the space in which others can make good decisions with far reaching effects – but *ultimately* (if indirectly) the success and welfare of the school is your responsibility. Mostly, however, you should aim to accept responsibility for what others have done. Being involved but not too involved is an interesting, if sometimes difficult, balance to achieve. A Chairman's role is not normally a highly creative one, but it can be very satisfying.

Methods of good communication

It is important that all governors are fully informed about the work of committees, either informally or through the termly meetings of the full board. Get your reporting process right: it underpins the overall plan, and governors must feel that they own it. In this way there is less risk of cliques developing within the board or a sense springing up of insiders and outsiders. The Chairman's role involves maintaining an open relationship with all the board's members; giving time to their individual concerns, and ensuring that they have information based on fact, not anecdote.

It may also be necessary from time to time for the Chairman, or individual governors at the Chairman's request, to listen to problems raised by parents or other interested parties, but only after these have been explored fully with the management. It is important to ensure that the governing body does not become a channel for going behind the Head's back.

Some boards have one or two members whose specific remit is to liaise with staff. They may simply be nominated from within the board's membership, or there may be a process whereby a nominee is elected by the staff. If the latter, the board should retain the power to reject unsuitable nominations, and in schools that are charities, employees and/ or beneficiaries of the charity are legally ineligible to sit on its governing body.[1] Thus a serving member of staff will be ineligible, whereas a former member is not ruled out. However the role is allocated, it is a potentially sensitive one. Those holding it should have clear terms of reference, as well as being aware of the need to keep the Head fully informed. The staff governor's most useful response to a concerned member of the common room is: "Have you already consulted the Head on this matter? If not, that should be your first step."

Getting the best out of people: a team effort

The Chairman should not try to take *everything* on to his or her own shoulders. One or more vice chairmen are there to be used, too – for example in chairing key committees or in taking soundings about succession planning for key roles on the board. It is important that there are formalised processes for succession planning and recruitment of *all* board members.

A board is often a somewhat random group of people in terms of personal chemistry: it needs to be nurtured and cultivated. Boards should aim to recruit not simply 'those we know', but 'those who will make a specific contribution, and with skills we currently lack'. Recruit the very best people you can and, having done so, make sure that they pull their weight. No board can afford to carry more than one or two passengers at most – and then only for a limited time. An attendance register will be a major help in determining who your passengers are. It is important, too, to achieve a balance of personalities. Avoid exposing the Head (especially if he or she is of a diffident disposition) to undue pressure from competing egos. A board comprised entirely of heavy-hitters can be a distinctly mixed blessing.

However, it is worth bearing in mind that large governing bodies can help to bind in big personalities. They are used to dealing with their kind, whereas if you have just one such in a board of otherwise meek and self-effacing people, there is a risk that he or she will dominate everything. They may be invaluable, too, as fundraisers, leading by example in the scale of their own giving and persuading others to do likewise.

Some schools raise funds through conventional appeals; some of the larger institutions develop permanent foundations to attract and retain potential major donors. A foundation can be a useful way to bind in energetic and successful people of means, whether they be governors or not, but the Chairman must then ensure that the foundation board never becomes a rival to, or substitute for, the governing body itself. The latter must always set the policy and the strategy, and the Head and bursar must be unequivocally accountable to the governors and no one else. There is much truth in the biblical saying that: 'No man can serve two masters.'

As Chairman, you are responsible for board discipline, and for ensuring that there is efficient liaison between key committees. This requires a cohesive overall team. My own experience has been that one of the best ways of achieving this is through the creation of the 'Chairman's Committee'. This consists of Chairman, vice chairmen (two, in the case of my own Board, respectively chairing the finance and general purposes and the education committees), along with the Head, the deputy head and the bursar. It operates less formally than the other committees, and meets at the start of each term to set the context for the three or four months ahead; collectively its members work to create a united sense of direction.

Some query the need for an education committee at all, believing that this is the management's area of expertise, and that the existence of such a group risks blurring the line between governance and management. My own view is that the education committee is an invaluable way of involving 'non-financial' governors in the board's committee work, and that this group has a key role in reviewing the quality of the 'product'. Many governors will come from an essentially non-educational background, even if they have been parents. A board's strategic plan should not be just about buildings and money, but should embrace academic policy, pastoral arrangements, inspection issues, and child protection matters.

Supporting the management team

As Chairman, you have one other key set of responsibilities: making sure that those whose job it is to develop and care for others are themselves cared for. Wise boards in any walk of life strive to look after their key employees. In a school, where the board has a large number of non-executive directors meeting two, perhaps three (if you include the Head, bursar and deputy head) executives it is especially important to nurture the executive arm.

School management is much more of a team effort than it once was, and in a sense you are the overseer of the team. At a formal level this means ensuring that the senior management team members all have reasonable contracts and other terms of employment; that they are formally appraised (preferably by a knowledgeable outsider, working closely with one or more governors), and that their salaries are properly reviewed each year, with appropriate guidance from the Head and bursar (see chapter 12).

Discussions concerning appraisal and remuneration should be carried out discreetly. They should be delegated by the board to a very small number of governors – either via a remuneration committee or the Chairman's committee as already described. Whatever method is used, the Chairman should consult one or two other governors along the way, rather than being the sole decision-maker; no one can see every aspect of a picture.

The Chairman also has an important, if less formal, part to play in the 'ongoing maintenance' of pastoral and other care for the senior team. It is often, and rightly, said that the Head's job is a lonely one. On the good days, the role is highly rewarding, but when times are harder, the Head soaks up many of the gripes, concerns and insecurities of others – the institution sometimes being blamed for the career or personal disappointments of the individual.

Even the best and outwardly most robust Head can suffer occasional bouts of sickness, loss of confidence or perspective, even serious illness. While as Chairman you are the line manager, you can also be critical friend and a sounding board, allowing the flying of kites and the airing of new ideas. Very few Heads will fail to appreciate the chance to unwind with their Chairman over a relaxed drink or a good meal.

Nearly everything written in the previous two paragraphs also applies to the bursar. While the Head is responsible to the board and the bursar to the Head, the best schools function through a creative, complementary triangular relationship between the Chairman and the two key senior managers. The Chairman and bursar may both have a great deal more business experience than the Head; the bursar may well have handled personnel, budgetary or procurement responsibilities in an earlier job on a far larger scale than in any school. The bursar should be seen as someone who is far more than just a finance director; the bursarial role involves extensive investment, property and human resources functions. In a financial or other crisis, it is the bursar who may have to be the whistleblower. The bursar who is also the clerk to the board has an additional role akin to being company secretary.

Bursars too can become isolated. When economic times are good they can be seen (especially by staff) as energetic enablers, but in times of downturn their role is often to trim budgets, creating a popular perception that 'can't be done' is the only phrase in their vocabulary. They too need concern and appreciation, especially from the Chairman.

One final thought

Even the very best boards in the most smoothly functioning schools are likely occasionally to experience bouts of turbulence: a poor appointment; high-profile publicity of the less desirable sort; a difficult disciplinary appeal; a controversial planning application. If in the good times the board has functioned well, and seemed reasonable and open to the varied constituencies that make up a school, it is far more likely when the going gets tough that people will give you the benefit of the doubt.

If, as Chairman, you have built that level of confidence and trust, you will have played a key role in sustaining the long-term reputation of your school, as well as doing a good and valuable job in determining its strategy and ensuring its effective performance.

References

1. Editors' note: this book went to press shortly after the publication of the report by Lord Carlile of Berriew, QC, into matters relating to Ealing Abbey and St Benedict's School, Ealing. In it he recommended that there should be a separate educational charity established for St Benedict's School – to include an elected staff representative and at least two parent representatives. He also recommended that the AGBIS 2011 *Guidelines for Governors* should be taken into account. The impact of this report on current practice remains to be seen, but current Charity Commission guidance suggests that it will only consider acceptable an employee as a trustee where it is clearly demonstrated that there is a substantial disadvantage in having the employee present only 'in attendance', rather than as a trustee.

Chapter 9

Building and developing the board

Richard Green

Between them the 1250 schools that are in membership of at least one of the associations within the Independent Schools' Council (ISC) have an estimated 15,000 governors. Thus there is a huge reservoir of talent to tap into. How can that talent be harnessed to create an effective board?

Over the past few years, AGBIS has conducted many reviews of governance of independent schools. From these, many common themes have emerged of issues that have caused boards to be less than effective, so lessons learned from these will be examined in the rest of this chapter:

- Selection of governors
- Too many nominated governors
- Inappropriate number of committees (too few, too many)
- No succession planning
- Poor governor awareness of responsibilities/training
- Uncertainty over future direction
- Confusion of responsibilities between the board and executive team
- No mechanism for review of board effectiveness

The size and composition of the board

As a general guide, the board should be of a size where the members between them are able to speak with knowledge and experience on the whole range of matters that are likely to come before them for decision. This suggests a minimum of ten members, to cover the range, and a maximum of 20, to foster involvement and active contribution from everyone. Some governing documents prescribe a larger number, in which case it may be efficient to make greater use of committees, each reporting to the board.

In looking at board composition, it is desirable to try to achieve a balance in a number of areas – for example, professional skills, age, gender, ethnicity – so that, taken as a whole, the board represents a broad spectrum of experience and views that can provide constructive challenge and debate. A balance also needs to be struck between introducing fresh blood and having governors with considerable experience (and therefore some 'corporate history'). At one end of the spectrum, if there is no continuity and the board changes, say, every three years, there may be a tendency towards short-termism. As a result, strategic planning may suffer. The converse, with little or no change in board composition, is that there can be a dearth of new ideas and challenge to the *status quo*.

Irrespective of any particular skill or background, the most pertinent question to ask of an existing or prospective governor is: 'Does s/he add value to the board?'

The skill areas that are most commonly sought for boards are:

- Education: a current or retired senior educationalist can assist the board's appreciation of the Head's job and can be a mentor to the Head.
- Business & finance: as so many decisions have a financial implication, it is essential that there is good business and financial expertise on the board to support and challenge the bursar.
- Property: many schools have significant property assets and invest in building projects. A governor experienced in property can provide valuable input to major decisions.
- Pastoral care: with children at the focal point of everything a school does, it is highly desirable to have a governor with a particular involvement in pastoral matters.
- Legal: many areas of a school's activities touch on areas where a lawyer's input would be of great value.
- ICT: a major investment area for many schools, and one where constructive challenge and advice are often needed.
- Marketing: particularly in smaller schools that cannot afford their

own fundraising and marketing departments, the contribution of an experienced marketer can make a valuable contribution to a school.

- HR management: with the increasing complexity of employment legislation, a pertinent question at the appropriate moment from an experienced HR professional could save the school a lot of money.
- Risk management: this is becoming increasingly important in the management of any enterprise: not just in health and safety, but also in areas such as reputation and financial management.
- Governance: the focus on governance within the charity sector has increased significantly; a governor experienced in charity trusteeship can help to ensure that best practice is followed.

Sometimes governors' talents lie hidden, so in the interests of trying to have a balanced board it is good practice to carry out a skills audit. It should be updated from time to time (perhaps every three years) to reflect the school's changing needs. One way of doing this is to draw up a matrix listing the skill areas the board requires, and identifying which members have primary or secondary experience in each of those areas.

An abbreviated example is shown below, listing governors' names on the left and showing just five of the possible skill areas across the top. Each governor is asked to state where s/he has primary (*ie* extensive) or secondary (*ie* some, but not in great depth) experience. Recording these as either 1 or 2, it is then possible from the table to identify where the board collectively has strength or needs to plug a gap.

	Education	Business	ICT	Property	Marketing
Brown	1		2		2
Jones		1		2	2
Marshall	2	2			2
Pearson		1		1	
Smith		2			1
Woods	2		2		
Young	1				

Identifying existing or prospective skills gaps is a useful step in prioritising future recruitment. It is generally easier to focus the search for new governors if there is a clear idea of the skills being sought. There are many sources of potential candidates – for example, the networks of governors, Head and bursar; the parent body; former pupils; local community links. Some schools have successfully recruited through advertising or non-executive websites. There is a view that advertising may be perceived as a sign of weakness, but in this increasingly transparent age it can be a strength to be seen to be looking for the best people available.

Other issues of balance

A balanced board is not just about skills. Ideally there should be a wide age range represented, but this often easier said than done as it can be difficult for younger candidates to find the time because of their family and career commitments. It may be worth holding board or committee meetings in evenings or at weekends, to enlarge the available pool of talent.

In all schools, whether single sex or coeducational, it is desirable that there should be board members of both sexes. Where a school has a significant proportion of pupils from ethnic minorities, the composition of the board should reflect that fact.

There are differing views on whether or not parents should serve as governors. The Board can benefit enormously from a direct contact with the school's 'customer base', and a parent governor is likely to have a strong interest in the school. There are potential conflicts of interest (for example, in fee setting) but these can be managed. However, a more difficult conflict to manage can arise where a parent has an issue with the Head or a member of staff over their pupil's education or discipline; some Heads and teachers find that knowing that the parent is also a governor adds pressure to what can be an awkward situation. It has also to be said that parent governor could use his/her position to exert undue influence on the member of staff. Some schools avoid these problems by appointing as governors parents of a child who has just left the school; the parent is still in touch with the school but is one stage removed from a potential conflict.

In any event, if a parent or former parent is to be a governor, s/he should be appointed on merit, as someone being able to contribute a useful skill to the board, and not as a representative of a factional interest group (such as a parents' association nominee). Where parents do form part of the board, their proportion should be a minority to avoid having a blocking, say, in major strategic decisions. Similar considerations apply in respect of former pupils, many of whom serve their old schools with energy and devotion.

Difficulties can arise where a school's constitution requires that a number of places on the board are to be filled by nomination from external bodies. There is often clear value to be had from close ties with other bodies and institutions, but sometimes their nominees are not able to devote the time or commitment to add value to the board's deliberations.

Having built a balanced board that adds value, how should it be best developed? First, beware of how the expert skills are used. Whilst it is very helpful to have a governor contributing professional expertise to a board discussion, it should be to challenge or supplement input from the senior management team or external advisers. It is tempting to use the skills of a professional on the board instead of paying for external advice when it is appropriate to do so (for example in a contentious issue, or where there is a lot of money at stake). There is a danger that if something goes wrong later the governor and board will be placed in an invidious position through having relied on that governor's judgement. By all means use a governor to act as devil's advocate but it is unfair on him/her if the board relies solely on his/her advice.

Succession planning and its importance
With a Board drawn from many constituent parts, it is unlikely (and undesirable) that its membership will remain static for long. Rather than be reactive – *ie* waiting until a resignation or departure –- it is best practice to have in place a succession plan, particularly for the Chairman and the chairmen of committees. No one will continue in a post indefinitely, and on occasions it can be embarrassing to deal with someone who has outstayed their welcome. A serving governor may also feel 'locked in' if there is no process whereby s/he can withdraw

gracefully. Many schools operate a system of retirement by rotation (typically three or five years) but more often than not such re-elections become automatic. It is therefore useful to have in place a clear understanding about the period of time that a governor should serve. This can be achieved by setting a maximum period of service (10-12 years is typical) or by encouraging retirement at a certain age, (say, 70-75) or a combination of the two. Doing more than 'encourage' might conflict with age discrimination legislation, following the removal of the default retirement age (the legal situation is not yet wholly clear), so a governing body would be unwise to try to stipulate age-related retirement without having taken legal advice.[1] There may, however, be circumstances where it is clearly in the interests of the school that a governor should serve beyond any generally accepted retirement age. This can be dealt with by trying informally to establish a convention of annual re-election after that age is reached.

By having a clear retirement plan, the board can plan ahead to replace the requisite skills. All too often boards fail to address one of the most crucial issues of all: the matter of chairmanship succession. Best practice suggests that the maximum term as Chairman should be no more than ten years, so that, with proper planning well in advance, steps can be taken to identify a successor. Very often, s/he will be an existing governor, but if there is not a suitable person available recruitment from outside may be necessary. Finding someone to fill this important role should be the responsibility of the board as a whole, although the detailed search may be delegated to an *ad hoc* group or (if there is one) to the governance/nominations committee. It may be that the board would not wish to advertise the position, as it may appear to be destabilising for the school; in such a case the use of a head hunter or other agency (such as AGBIS) may be worthwhile.

Induction and training of board members
For the board to be effective, governors need to be well versed in the general principles of trusteeship and get up to speed quickly on the dynamics of the school. A thorough induction process should pay dividends rapidly in the governor being able to add value. Much of this

should be done face-to-face, with the bursar/clerk to the governors, the Head and the Chairman. Typical topics that might be covered include:

- the school's strategic plan;
- the main issues facing the school;
- roles and responsibilities of governors;
- the governance structure;
- the school's financial position;
- performance assessment of the school, the Head, the SMT, the board.

It can also be useful having a 'buddy governor' whereby a new member of the board is assigned to mentor an existing governor for, say, a year, so that the new appointee has a specific individual to call on whilst becoming familiar with the school. There is invariably a lot of background reading that can be given to a new governor. At the end of this chapter is a suggested list of the information that could be made available, although the requirements for each school will be different.

After induction, there is an ongoing need for keeping up-to-date with relevant changes in practice and regulation. Many organisations, including AGBIS, offer seminars for governors, but it is not always easy for governors to attend courses. Some boards hold in-house training, timed to take place immediately before or after a board meeting, when an external facilitator can provide a tailored update on recent developments. AGBIS is making a significant investment in e-learning, both for the induction of new governors and for more advanced training aimed at those with some experience. It is hoped that, by making training more accessible and in line with current practice in industry generally, those with heavy commitments elsewhere will be able more readily to offer themselves as governors.

The board and its constituent parts
With the board fully inducted and trained, what other practicalities are there in developing it? One of the consequences of having relatively infrequent board meetings (typically one a term) is that it is important to keep governors informed of significant activities in the intervening periods: for example, circulating details of external exam results,

newsletters to parents and invitations to school events keeps governors aware of what is going on at the school.

The Chairman is likely to be more closely involved than other governors in working with and advising the Head and bursar on issues as they arise from time to time. Knowing the strengths and skills of fellow governors, the Chairman is well placed to suggest to the Head or bursar where advice may be sought from a board member on a particular matter.

Most boards function with one or more committees. There can be no hard and fast rules about which committees to have, but, as a guide, the most common ones are:

- Finance
- Estates
- Education
- Governance/nominations

Typical issues that might be covered by these committees include:

Finance: Budgets, termly management accounts, financial control procedures, debt collection, banking arrangements, approval of audited accounts, recommending fee levels, salary structures.

Estates: Monitoring major repair projects, overseeing development projects, health & safety in relation to the school's physical infrastructure.

Education: Reviewing admissions policy, public exam results, curriculum development, extracurricular activities, teaching staff levels, pastoral care, school policies, H&S as it affects pupils and staff.

Governance: Reviewing composition of board (balance), governor appointment and induction, nominations and induction, governor training, board succession planning, recruitment/remuneration and appraisal of Head and bursar, procedures for regulatory and legal compliance.

Whilst this committee structure is likely to be sufficient for the average sized school, it may be too cumbersome for a small school and insufficient for a large one. The scope of the ubiquitous finance and general purposes (F&GP) committee often encompasses much of what is covered in finance, estates and governance/nominations and can be suitable for a smaller school. There is, though, a risk that it can reduce the role of the board; a governor not on the F&GP could therefore feel marginalised if all the key matters have been dealt with by the F&GP.

In larger schools, four committees may not be enough to support the board in running effectively. Where, for example, there is a junior school run by the same board, it is likely to be desirable that there should be a junior school committee to work with its Head on issues affecting it. Ultimately though, it will be for each individual board to decide what committees it requires. The list below shows some of the areas where schools have used other committees:

- Marketing
- Investment
- Audit/risk
- Bursaries
- Capital projects
- Remuneration
- Strategic planning.

To enable all governors, wherever possible, to play a full part, it is usual for all members of the board to serve on at least one committee. This provides them with the opportunity to become involved in detail in some areas of the school's governance. Experience has shown though that some governors (*eg* nominated or serving Heads of other schools) may not have the time available to devote to committee meetings. Their contributions at board level are still, of course, of great value and they can perform the useful role of acting as a counterbalance in seeing the wood for the trees.

Territorial responsibility, and terms of reference
It is important to determine the split of responsibility between the board (non-executive) and the Head (executive). Take, for example, marketing. Many smaller schools do not have their own marketing department but their boards may contain governors with marketing experience. It can be tempting for those with specialist expertise to apply their knowledge in a very hands-on way, to the point of overriding or excluding the Head in

important decisions. They should limit their involvement to advice, but if they take too active a role this can act as a disincentive to the employed staff and can blur accountabilities if things should go wrong.

Whilst there may be a number of standing committees covering areas listed above, from time to time a board may find it useful to convene an *ad hoc* working group to deal with a specific issue – for example, a building project or a fundraising appeal. These groups should have a defined purpose, terms of reference and, importantly, a predefined cut-off point so that once the mission has been accomplished the group is disbanded: otherwise there is otherwise the risk that what started as *ad hoc* turns out to be ongoing, and clutters up the committee structure.

A governor with particular expertise in the respective area should chair the relevant committee, and those committees should be used to help the board function more effectively by dealing in more depth with matters within their purview. It is important that each committee has clear terms of reference and that its role is seen as supporting and, where necessary, challenging the executive team, to whom the running of the school is delegated. It is useful to programme committee meetings in a cycle that leads (usually towards the end of a term) into a board meeting, at which the board can consider major recommendations and reports from those committees. To ensure that those board members who are not on a particular committee can have the opportunity of understanding the issues dealt with at committee level, many schools include copies of all committee papers as an appendix to their board meeting papers. The next few chapters describe the workings of some of these committees in greater detail.

Periodically, the board should review its own performance and that of its committees, to ensure that its governance structure remains relevant and that the best use is being made of the skills available. AGBIS offers reviews of governance to its members and has on its website a suggested programme for performance self-review.

Suggested information for governor induction

Documents for general information and guidance to governors:

- AGBIS *Guidelines for Governors*
- CC60 *Hallmarks of an Effective Charity*
- CC3 *The Essential Trustee*
- *Good Governance – Summary Code*
- Training courses available

Information specific to the school:

- Memorandum and Articles of Association (or equivalent constitution)
- Most recent audited accounts and management accounts
- School policy documents (including child protection and financial controls)
- Board and committee terms of reference
- Schedule of governors' meetings
- Membership of governors' committees
- Minutes of board of governors and appropriate committees
- Strategic development plan
- Business risk analysis
- Most recent inspection report
- School prospectus
- Staff list
- Governors' contact details
- Termly calendar

References

1. The Editors are very gradeful to Sarah McKimm, Principal Solicitor (Education and Children) at ISC, for advice on this point.

Chapter 10

Estates, finance, general purposes and audit committees

Gerald Ellison

Some schools may well group the quartet of components in this chapter heading into the terms of reference for a single committee. Others may spread them over two or three; a few may have separate committees for each of the four. However, whatever the arrangements of your school, the same essential areas need to be covered, and all the committees need to have their respective roles well defined and well linked well together, with clear terms of reference. The responsibility of each should be correlated with the school's risk management schedule.

A fundamental responsibility of governors (particularly those that are also charity trustees) is to ensure that the value of the school's assets is maintained. There is also an expectation that governors will improve and maximise the value of those assets, the better to meet the aims of the school.

The estates committee
Land and buildings are the principal assets of most schools, so the estates committee needs to:

- Consider the adequacy of the school's land and buildings for the needs of the school (actual and planned).
- Receive and review a regular condition survey of the school's buildings.
- Review regular reports on the value of the school's buildings for rebuilding purposes and ensure that the value is reflected in the school's insurance policies.

- Review regular reports on the value of school's land and buildings for disposal under current use, and for development.
- Ensure that the school takes the opportunity to influence changes in the local planning environment – particularly with regard to the planning designation of its land.

These are key areas for governors: part of their strategic role. Master-planning is also a valuable tool to them – unless, of course, they are one of those rare schools that is certain that it has all the facilities it needs for the foreseeable future. However, most do not, and the bad news about master-planning is that it is not a one-off exercise. The process of review of a school's strategic plan starts almost as soon as the plan has been completed: it is a continual process. Master-planning needs similar reassessment.

The good news is that a master-plan does not (unless there are exceptional circumstances) need re-doing more than every five or ten years – and often less frequently – although it should be tested annually against a school's changing needs. The important thing is that the estates committee should be confident that year-on-year development is consistent with the longer-term plan for the school's site and buildings.

When it comes to detailed decisions over building development – new-build, extension or refurbishment – there are different governance approaches, often determined by the level of skill within a school's management, and its experience of managing development projects. There are, however, some absolute requirements of the estates' committee. These include setting a financial limit for the size of contracts that can be agreed by management without separate authority from governors; establishing a mechanism for reporting the results of tenders; and agreeing a format for reporting the outturn of contract costs against budget. Although not a requirement as such, it is also good practice for the same committee to be aware of the progress of planning applications made by the school.

The extent of governors' involvement in decisions over design, procurement, and project management will usually follow established practice in each school, and will probably vary according to the scale and nature of the development. It is, however, important for that practice to be understood and agreed, and for the committee to receive the necessary reports for it to be able to exercise the control that it has determined to be appropriate.

Other areas that can be usefully addressed by the estates committee include health & safety (H&S); green policies; security and lettings. H&S responsibilities and mechanisms for addressing them were discussed in chapter 3, but it is worth reiterating that governors have an obligation to ensure that the school meets the H&S requirements placed on it – both as a matter of good practice and through statutory requirements such as the Independent School Regulations, Corporate Manslaughter Act, *etc.*

Details of governors' 'green' policies (a term that covers the construction of energy efficient buildings, energy management, recycling, travel plans and the school's carbon footprint) are matters of increasing public interest and often play a part in the gaining of planning approvals. Schools therefore need to keep abreast of green issues. There are also clear cost benefits to managing energy efficiently. However, taking a green approach to everything is often not the cheapest option in the short term, and the longer-term benefits of some innovations are yet to be proved in practice. Each school will have its own view on the cost/value benefit of different measures and will determine the extent to which it wishes to implement green policies. It is a changing world and what is inappropriate to a school's circumstances one year may be appropriate the next year. An annual report to the committee is helpful in enabling governors to remain informed and to keep matters under review.

Security – of property and person – is a concern for all schools and is an area considered under ISI inspections. It can be worked into the governors' review of H&S and should be covered by school's risk management process. However, a separate annual report to the estates committee on measures to maintain security and on its response to incidents that have breached or threatened security during the past year is good practice.

Lettings may at first sight seem to be mainly a financial issue for governors, as opposed to an estates one. This is particularly true where there are significant specialist facilities – for example, a sports or performing arts centre with a high degree of commercial operation, or where a school's general buildings are able to support a high turnover from conferences or weddings. Schools with lesser facilities will still seek to generate external revenue from them – through language schools, holiday camps, sports clubs, music rehearsals and master-classes, lectures and seminars. No matter what the scale, lettings are an important source of income, and they rightly come within the purlieu of a finance committee.

All that said, however, the requirements of fire and other H&S regulations, disability discrimination legislation, licensing law, and insurance, necessitate more than purely financial considerations. Schools need a policy both on the extent to which they should involve themselves in non-core activities, and on the balance between commercial leverage and provision of community and public benefit. The estates committee needs to be aware of the pressure that lettings place on the wear and tear of premises, and also of the restrictions that they place on the school's ability to maintain the very facilities that it lets. There is also the matter of design: how much, for example, should community and commercial use be built into plans for a new building?

The finance committee

Governors' responsibility for a school's assets applies more widely than to those visible assets represented by land and buildings. It is to the governors' finance committee that the board usually looks for the development and monitoring of the school's strategy on assets as a whole.

Recent changes in charity law have allowed greater flexibility in the treatment of endowed funds, which should see a decline in those numerous small charitable funds with static capital and declining real-terms income, and should encourage investment in vehicles appropriate to a charity's purpose. Simultaneously there has been a growth in acceptance by donors of the principle of expendable endowment (and the greater use of designated rather than restricted funds), which has greatly aided the funding of bursaries in many schools. It is *not* a change from 'what I have, I hold' conservatism to 'making assets sweat' in the way of aggressive arbitrageurs, but it is one that puts a proper onus on governors to ensure that a school's assets are actively, while still prudently, managed for the benefit of the school.

Active responsibility for a school's assets means much more than ensuring effective management of property and endowed funds. Schools need to determine the level of reserves that it is appropriate for them to hold, to support their activities and to provide reasonable measure of comfort against bad times. The key word here is 'appropriate': building and holding reserves merely for their own sake is not appropriate, especially as (for most schools) this can only be done by retaining surpluses generated from fee income. Parents accept that part of the fees they pay go to provide facilities or bursaries or to improve the financial soundness of the school for future generations in the same way that their children benefit from the same approach having been taken by previous generations of parents. They will not accept a situation where reserves are being increased by the accumulation of surpluses to no established purpose. Schools need to justify their level of surplus.

Oversight of a surplus and reserves strategy is a key responsibility of a finance committee. Although this may sound too theoretical for a school that is struggling to produce the income necessary to meet its expenditure, a strategy on reserves and surplus is as important (arguably more so) for a school in trouble as for any other school.

How does a finance committee ensure that such a strategy, once agreed, is being delivered? The first step, as ever, is the setting of a budget consistent with the strategy.

Setting the budget involves setting fees, and governors need to assure themselves that the level of fees can be borne by the market. The finance committee needs to be aware of broad economic conditions affecting the school's market, and to see current fees benchmarked against those of similar and competitor schools. The Competition Act does not prevent a school from carrying out such an exercise from publicly available information for its own use. Governors (or possibly the board or finance committee Chairman, on the board's behalf) will also need to approve a draft letter to parents giving an honest and cogent explanation to parents of the proposed fees.

Budgets are as much about expenditure as income. Governors should require the management to benchmark the school's previous performance against sector surveys, and (assuming that benchmarking has not thrown up major questions) to ensure that material variances from the previous year's expenditure are explained within a commentary on the budget. This commentary should set out proposed changes to staffing levels and salary scales, and should detail proposed capital expenditure, all of which should be subject to approval by the committee. A cash flow and balance sheet projection should form part of the budget papers.

The second step is by measuring performance against budget. Most schools report this to the finance committee termly. As with the budget, the report should include: an income and expenditure account; balance sheet and cash flow reconciliation; a commentary explaining variances; a projected outturn for the year and the prior year's comparative figures. All governors need to understand a school's financial performance, but some tend to be more used to the formal presentation of accounting information than others. An effective solution is for income and expenditure (I&E), balance sheet and cash flow to be presented in a traditional accounting manner; the commentary should be detailed but with an 'executive summary'; and, drawn from the figures, key performance indicators (KPIs) should be included. These may include:

- Fee income
- Total income
- Staffing costs
- Total operating costs
- Operating surplus
- Depreciation (can be shown within operating costs)
- Interest payments (can be shown within operating costs)
- Total surplus
- Capital expenditure
- Pupil numbers
- Staff numbers
- Pupil: staff ratio
- Bank borrowing, and how bank covenants are being met.

Many of these can be shown best as a percentage of another figure (*eg* staffing costs as a percentage of fee income), as well as in simple number form. All the figures benefit from being shown with the current year's projected outturn compared to budget and the last five years performance, so that governors can see and monitor the trends.

In their simplest form annual audited accounts are an external confirmation of the termly accounts, albeit with the addition of some details and notes required by the Companies Act that may be superfluous to the presentation of termly accounts. Where the presentation of termly accounts differs from that of annual accounts, reconciliation between the two should be provided.

There must be a clear remit to the most appropriate committee of the Board to cover the audit role: the appointment of external auditors; agreement of the scope of the annual audit; review of the audit process, and consideration of the audit management letter. These will be dealt with in the final section of this chapter, on the audit committee, along with internal audit matters (reviews of the procedures and effectiveness of particular cost areas or functions within the school), insurance, and risk management. However, a majority of schools do not have an audit committee as such, and include its role in that of the finance committee.

Banking arrangements are another important finance committee responsibility. Day-to-day banking arrangements are a relatively minor matter, but borrowing from, and investing surplus cash with, banks (and most schools do both) are greater ones.

Before the recent banking crisis the major concern of schools seeking loan or overdraft finance was to achieve the lowest possible interest rate – and there were some spectacularly low ones around, as banks competed for sector business. Banks still do this, but the interest rates they offer are of a different order. More importantly, schools' attitude towards borrowing has had to change. If a school is dependent on loan finance, the interest rate on offer is less important than the security of the funding. Put simply, the guaranteed term of the loan needs to meet the period of the school's need for the funding provided by it. Whether the loan has a fixed or variable rate, and, if variable, whether it should be hedged, capped or otherwise protected, are matters for individual schools and their circumstances.

Most schools, even those with bank loans will, by virtue of the advance payment of school fees, have surplus cash during a year. Managing this surplus cash well has always been good practice. With the current fragility of banks (with which surplus cash tends to be invested) the need to protect the investment has increased in importance over the return to be gained from it (a mirror image of borrowing).

The finance committee, while still examining the cost of funds, needs to assure itself of the availability of funds, and that the school can meet the covenants applied to a loan (see earlier, re KPI). The committee also needs to assure itself that deposited cash is as secure as it can be: even where funds are small, it would be wise to adopt a treasury management policy.

The relatively few schools that have a significant endowment beyond the value of land and buildings and therefore invested in other vehicles will be aware of the need to have an investment policy and for that policy to be managed effectively. If there is not a separate investment committee, responsibility for reviewing investments and investment policy is most likely to fall to the finance committee; similarly, bursary policy and, in smaller schools, bursary awards.

Finally, the committee needs to ensure that reporting requirements – particularly to the Charities Commission and Companies House – are met. It should also consider regular benchmarking that extends well beyond fees, to measure its school's performance against others in areas of particular interest or concern.

Separate or combined

Should there be separate estates and finance committees? I suggest not – unless a school has wholly exceptional issues with, or portfolios of, land and buildings. It is difficult to think of estates work that doesn't have a significant financial implication: master-planning; building projects; the sale, acquisition and development of land; even the maintenance programme. It seems poor use of governors' time to have two meetings each concentrating on different aspects of the same matter rather than discuss them as a whole. Most governors are generalists by experience and outlook, even if professionally they are specialists, and they want to see things in the round. The volume of business that a combined estates and finance committee needs to address is large, but that should not be an obstacle to their combination. Not everything has to be considered at every meeting – reports can be annual, biennial or triennial, so long as all areas are covered appropriately to the circumstances of the school and the legal requirements placed on it. The onus is on the school's management to provide succinct reports, with executive summaries and supporting papers.

That said, a board with a joint estates and finance committee must avoid giving a sense to other governors that it is an inner circle: a board within a board. While a communicative and effective board Chairman (who should be an ex-officio member of the committee) will prevent this, a separate audit committee, the majority of whose members should not also be members of the estates and finance committee, will help to avoid such a sense arising.

General purposes

Rather than having a committee with a purely financial remit, many schools have an F&GP committee (finance and general purposes: an acronym understood for several years by the daughter of one colleague to be the 'effing GP'). The longer title is fine, but in reality GP is anachronistic, left over from a lazier time when schools didn't trouble themselves overmuch with committees' specific responsibilities and accountabilities, and needed a vehicle for subjects that had been otherwise unaddressed.

Schools should have a governance structure with the appropriate committees for their needs and with terms of reference that make 'general purposes' a redundant catch-all. If all the subjects mentioned earlier in this chapter are covered by an estates and/or finance committee (with audit, investment, and bursary committees as required) and schools have other committees according to their needs (education, nominations, marketing and development), I struggle to think what could be left to 'general purposes'. Exceptional circumstances arise – the need to appoint a new Head; to oversee a large project, *etc* – but these are better handled by a temporary committee or sub-committee than being sloughed off under a 'general purposes' heading.

This view is born out of the belief that, although all governors are responsible for all decisions of the board, there is nothing that should come to the board (which, in most schools, meets formally once a term and annually for little more than six hours) that has not already been discussed in detail by one of its committees. How else can the board as a whole exercise its duties and conduct its business effectively?

The audit committee

A few years ago, in the wake of the Higgs Report on corporate governance and the accompanying Smith Report on audit committee reform, there was a seemingly endless stream of briefing notes on audit committees in independent schools. At the time only a minority of schools had an audit committee. Governors with large company, higher education or major non-governmental organisation experience tended to press for their introduction; legal and accounting sector specialists were divided between the pro and anti camps, or rather unhelpfully, sat on the fence; schools and boards were understandably confused.

In the way of such matters, the stream of advice and articles – and the debate within boards – dried up as the sector's attention was drawn elsewhere. I suspect that audit committees have proliferated, but whether or not to have an audit committee remains an important decision for governors.

The main question to be considered is this: is the role of an audit committee carried out effectively (or as effectively as it might be) by other committees? Herein lies a common problem because the audit committee's role is often misunderstood – more often than not by those discussing its possible introduction, and nowhere more so than when looking at the respective roles of the finance and the audit committees in the matter of the annual audit and financial statements.

So firstly, a little on the distinction between the two committees in this area: the audit committee looks primarily at process. It is concerned with the external audit report on the school's financial statements; the extent and effectiveness of the external auditors' work; the external auditors' management letter. The audit committee is *not* concerned with the financial statements in terms of how they reflect the financial performance and position of the school. The figures in the financial statements themselves are not a subject for discussion for the audit committee: they are sent to the audit committee so as to provide a context for the external audit report, the work of the auditors and the management letter.

This is the reverse of the role of the finance committee, which looks at the financial performance and position of the school while receiving the external audit report and management letter (approved by the audit committee) so as to provide background and context to the financial statements.

Can one committee look at both process and detail? Yes: but it is far more effective governance, and accepted better practice, for the roles to be split. This distinction between process and detail applies equally to the important area of risk management, where both the audit committee and the finance committee again have different roles.

It is a whole board responsibility to consider the major risks to which a school is exposed and the systems designed to mitigate those risks. In reality, as in so many other areas, the board needs to delegate to its committees a large amount of the practical work so that it does not get weighed down by detail and has sufficient time to exercise genuine oversight. An effective allocation of tasks in terms of risk management is for the audit committee to concentrate on reviewing the risk management process and satisfying itself that the process encompasses all the risks likely to be faced by the school, leaving the finance committee to carry out a detailed review of the management of individual risks.

Apart from the annual financial audit and risk management (albeit, two key areas) what other responsibilities can the audit committee bear to the benefit of the board? Where else can it bring value? Some specific areas are:

- Reviewing the school's fulfilment of its charitable purpose by ensuring that its activities are consistent with its charitable object as set out in its Memorandum of Association (and that they are for the public benefit).

- Reviewing the critical incident plan.
- Reviewing measures to conform to the requirements of the Bribery Act.
- Reviewing the board's committee and group structure.
- Ensuring that a regular appraisal or self-appraisal (ideally using an external facilitator) of the governing board takes place, and that annually governors have an opportunity to comment on the operation of the board (perhaps via a short questionnaire).

More generally, the audit committee can be used to consider the financial *and non-financial* operational and management controls and to recommend to the board an audit of any such area or areas. Examples of such areas include: non-teaching-staff pension management; investment management; catering; ICT and lettings. The audit committee should have a free remit to look into any area that it believes merits particular attention.

All these tasks could in theory be carried out by the finance committee, but only at the very real risk of overload – especially if the finance committee also has estates responsibilities. This could result in the tasks not being carried out in sufficient depth.

In other words: can an effective governing board afford *not* to have an audit committee?

Chapter 11

The education committee

Joy Richardson

Who needs an education committee?

Governing bodies vary in their committee structure, but all have full board meetings and almost all have some form of committee to oversee money and property, often with the catch-all title of 'Finance and General Purposes'. Traditionally, in many schools, governors busied themselves with the business side of the enterprise, where many had expertise, leaving education to the school's SMT. This was seen as a way to avoid overstepping the closely guarded line between governance and management.

Life has moved on, secret gardens have been opened up and thinking has changed. Most schools large enough to have a formal committee structure have now instigated an education committee in some form. It may be cast as an education committee, an academic advisory committee or, in some schools, a teaching and learning committee. Its purpose is to provide effective oversight of the school's core work and to ensure that board decisions are fully informed by the consideration of educational implications. The education committee helps to fulfil governors' responsibility to support and challenge, with a more detailed focus on academic matters than can be achieved at the full board.

A good starting point is to consider the declared aims of the school. These usually focus on educational outcomes, high standards, all-round learning and personal development. It is the job of the education committee to hold the school to account in precisely these areas. If governors know the school's financial status and its building plans, but have no sense of why its exam results are as they are, or of the impact of decisions about staffing or pastoral care, governance will be lopsided.

That which is focused on becomes that which is important, and the governing body should make clear that educational outcomes for pupils are central to its vision.

Terms of reference

The education committee, however named, should be clear about its purpose and the limits of its purview. Essentially, it should exercise a monitoring and advisory role in respect of the school's academic, curricular and pastoral provision. Its remit is wide in encompassing all aspects of the school's educational mission, and helping to shape its academic strategy. To fulfil its function it should seek to develop an overview of the school's educational performance. This requires a broad understanding of the nature and diversity of its intake, and of its curricular, extracurricular and examination programmes. The committee should contribute time and insight in evaluating pupils' academic success, the quality of their broader educational experience and the provision of pastoral care. It should also play its part, on behalf of the governing body, in reviewing policies and procedures to ensure compliance and effective implementation.

Clear terms of reference are required. These should carefully navigate that tricky line between governance and management. The committee is essentially a sounding board for management, with an advisory rather than a decision-making role, although it might on occasions be required to bring forward recommendations to the board in areas it has been mandated to consider.

Terms of reference should be reviewed annually to ensure that the committee's purpose is being well served. This should be done in conjunction with scrutiny of the terms of reference for other committees to minimise overlap and to ensure that no key areas of the school's work fall between the cracks. Who, for example, should be asking questions about the marketing department, the staffing of the health centre or the quality of boarding care?

An important area that is too often skirted around by governors is the relationship between staffing costs (far and away the largest element of any school budget) and educational effectiveness. Clearly, scrutiny of the budget falls within the remit of the finance committee, and governors should not delve too deeply into operational decisions about set sizes or GCSE options. Yet an education committee should be expected to ask challenging questions about the rationale behind staff deployment. For example, the pupil:teacher ratio in independent schools has fallen steadily in recent years, thus contributing to fee increases. Governors should understand why, and what this has achieved, and the educational implications of belt tightening if times become harder. Careful coordination is needed to ensure balanced scrutiny of the educational and financial implications of development plans, whether in the context of growth, or downsizing.

The board has a legal responsibility to ensure that the school's policies and procedures comply with the legal requirements for independent schools. There should be clear guidance to committees about which policies they are responsible for reviewing on a regular cycle. The terms of reference should spell out the oversight expected from the education committee of educational and pastoral policies, with a particular emphasis on safeguarding, behaviour and discipline and anti-bullying. The committee should ensure the required annual reporting to the board on the working of the child protection policy.

Structure and membership

The Head, and usually another member of the senior management team such as the academic deputy or the director of studies, should be in regular attendance and play a major part in shaping the agenda. No education committee can function unless properly serviced by the school's management. However, as a governors' committee reporting to the full board, it is not appropriate for it to be chaired by a member of the school's staff, even the Head.

Governors' succession planning should extend to the chairmanship and membership of committees in order to maintain a balanced and coherent structure. It is useful to have an expectation that most, if not all, governors serve on one or other of the principal committees, and it should be established on appointment whether this will be possible: for example, retired Heads are more likely than serving Heads to offer this level of commitment. Committee membership can be quickly eroded if too many governors are unable to manage more than the termly board meeting. The terms of reference should set a quorum in order to ensure a reasonable turnout, though some flexibility may be advisable if the focus is on advice rather than decision-making. It may also be appropriate to co-opt members from outside the governing body in order to strengthen the committee's membership.

While governors with an educational background are the obvious choice for education committee membership, some crossover of expertise is advisable. Whether in the financial or the educational arena, a governor from another field can bring fresh air to the discussion. It is healthy sometimes to go back to first principles in asking why things are as they are, as well as considering how they can be improved. All committees need someone with the knack of asking – at the right moment – the deceptively simple question. It may make the experts roll their eyes, but it can lead to a bracing discussion that ultimately reaches the heart of the matter.

While very small schools may not need a separate education committee, many larger schools face the question of whether a single committee can serve the needs of different parts of the schools. Where there are separate junior and senior schools, or preps, pre-preps and nurseries, separate committees may be needed, although a joint meeting, perhaps once a year, can help to focus on issues of continuity and transition. Some schools adopt a pattern of focusing on a different section of the school in each meeting alongside some consideration of whole-school issues.

An education committee is only able to function effectively if it has a clear remit; if meetings are scheduled well in advance as part of the whole cycle of governors' meetings, and if its work is fully integrated with that of other committees and the full Board. The chairman of the committee should work closely with the chairman of the finance committee and the Chairman of governors to ensure that these conditions are met.

The scope of the committee's work
Many schools produce an academic report or review that can form the substance of the committee's work at its meeting in the autumn term.

This gives the opportunity for broad-ranging discussion of the school's academic direction and any new initiatives, and for the scrutiny of performance in external exams. Many schools also produce measures of progress and targets for attainment, which help to set sights high. Governors should know the headlines and make sure that they understand the big picture, without becoming bogged down in detail. Where expectations have not been met, questions need to be asked, but these should seek elucidation and explanation, rather than appearing to rush to judgement.

The bulk of the work by governors will be done in reading the report beforehand, so that lines of questioning are pertinent and well judged. A good assumption is that any major trend or anomaly in performance will have been picked up by the management team so the committee should tap into their thinking and ask for elaboration. The main focus should be on finding the way forward rather than picking over the past. Governors let loose on a set of statistics may be tempted to parade their perspicacity in pointing out errors or cavilling over typos. This is best done outside the meeting.

Some, but not all, schools have a strong system of school development or improvement planning. Where this is the case, goals are set out on an annual basis, usually within a longer three or five year framework. The development plan is more than a mission statement, and more than a wish list of building projects. It should include the school's educational priorities and identified areas for improvement. When properly drawn up, with wide involvement of staff and governors, it becomes the school's engine house. Agreed objectives can be referred back to during the appraisal or performance management of staff and of the leadership team. The process links to the school's self-evaluation in which governors' should also play a role.

A strong school development plan provides a conduit for governors' questions and should be referred to at every meeting, to evaluate the progress being made. This provides a sense of direction and continuity and avoids causes for concern, or items for the agenda, being plucked from the air. If, for example, the introduction of the IB or the extension of a learning support programme is an agreed priority for the year, this will help to determine the areas in which governors seek updates or receive presentations from staff. In this cyclical pattern, the annual report provides a summary of progress towards previously agreed goals and helps to map out the action needed in the coming year. Consideration of the development plan also focuses governors on their role in securing an effective appraisal system, and ensuring the continuing professional development of the staff and the leadership team, including the Head.

The education committee, on behalf of the governing body, plays a major part in reviewing policies and procedures and ensuring that they are fit for purpose and legally compliant. There should be a clear understanding of which policies are reviewed in which committee, and how and when this is done. The responsibility is one of oversight: it is the job of the management, not of governors, to write policies. It may be helpful for a member of the committee to be designated as child protection governor, to facilitate liaison with the school's named person in this important area. However, the responsibility remains collective and an individual governor nominee is not a legal requirement.

Working with the leadership team

This committee is the one on which the school's educational leaders feel most at home, and yet where their expertise can feel most threatened. It can also add to their workload without adding value to their work. An education committee should aim to be paper light, and its paperwork should draw on that which has to be produced anyway as part of the school's cycle of planning. Casual demands for 'a paper on...' should be avoided.

The education committee should be a source of support to the Head and senior team. The very fact of spending time on discussing educational issues gives recognition that these are important. The committee can also be a sounding board. The Head should be free to fly kites and to gauge the reaction, or to prepare the ground for future discussion. It is helpful to reserve part of the meeting for the Head to share issues that are currently at the top of the leadership team's agenda, or to flag up developments beyond the school that will have an impact internally. As a general rule, there should be more governors than members of staff in attendance, or it simply becomes an extension of a senior management team meeting. At the same time, it is important that senior staff gain experience of working with governors, particularly if they are on a trajectory leading to headship.

Governors help to bring the outside world into the school, but they also need to be informed about the outside world of schools, in order better to understand the school's own context. Committee members with an educational background can be invaluable in giving a wider perspective so long as they do not offer their own experience as the only benchmark.

Governors with a close emotional connection to the school need to exercise particular care on an education committee to ensure that their contribution is informed, but not overbalanced, by their personal experience. Current parents in particular should be wary of taking up causes in committee that are especially pertinent to their children: the hat change from parent to governor should take place at the door.

Presentations from staff

The education committee can provide a bridge between the governing body and the teaching staff by focusing on what ultimately matters most: the education of pupils. It is supported in this by receiving presentations from staff. These may take the form of a site visit: for example, to see how resources are being used for the teaching of modern languages, or how the geography department is making use of IT, or to view arrangements in the nursery.

It is valuable for governors physically to walk the patch, particularly when the use of facilities is at issue. How well are space and resources being used, and what are the constraints? On other occasions, it may be more time efficient for governors to receive a presentation in their meeting room about a subject department or other aspect of school life. In this case, it is helpful if the member of staff concerned is able to circulate a brief paper before the meeting to ensure that the time available (typically 30 minutes or so) is used to full effect and includes opportunity for questions and discussion.

It is realistic to aim for between three and six visits or presentations over the course of, probably, three meetings a year. There may also be the chance to meet socially with designated groups of staff or pupils – new heads of department or boarding house staff, prefects or members of the school council – before, during or after the meeting. If the school has several sections, it is important over time to ensure that none falls beneath the radar. Benign neglect is rarely appreciated as such.

A careful record should be kept of whom the committee met, when, and regular review of this list helps to pinpoint areas and departments that have had little attention. The programme of presentations should be planned in advance, but not too far in advance. The Head will have views on whom it might be helpful to meet and when, and may well want to delay a meeting when departmental leadership is about to change, or to bring forward a presentation about a new initiative.

The committee should always check out before a presentation whether there are particular lines of questioning that it would be useful to pursue, to help governors to relate what they hear to the bigger picture of school development.

The work of the finance and the education committees should be seen as two sides of the governing coin. The teaching of new subjects or the refurbishing of science labs; the extension of a pre-prep building or an increase in class size all have educational as well as financial implications. A marketing or fundraising strategy cannot be successful without a clear view of educational quality. Wherever possible, the agenda of the education committee and the presentations it receives should help to inform the finance committee about the educational implications of its decisions, and *vice versa*.

Maximising effectiveness
An education committee, along with other committees of the governing body, should regularly evaluate its own effectiveness. Above all, is it providing value for time? Meetings need to fit into a tidy and regular structure so that, for example, the education committee has a regular slot towards the beginning of the term, followed by the finance committee and then by the full governing body meeting towards the end of the

term. Additional committees or working parties should be appended to these meetings so that dates do not proliferate. Two hours or so is long enough for an education committee, allowing time for communication by the Head, updating on development priorities and one or two sharply scheduled presentations or visits.

School calendars are set a long way ahead, and all governors' meetings should be scheduled at least a year in advance. Short notice changes of date are irritating for everyone and can imply an *ad hoc* approach. If a change is unavoidable, all governors should be informed, and preferably consulted. The distribution or emailing of paperwork a week before the meeting helps proper preparation (though the 'paper or screen' debate still has some way to run). Responsibility for this, and for taking minutes, should be part of a specific work allocation so that committee members have a single administrative point of reference.

The Chairman of the governors may choose to sit on the committee, but should in any case keep in close contact with the committee Chairman. The aim is to integrate the work of the committees into the board's decision-making processes. The work of the committee should be reported to the board through the circulation of its minutes. At the full board, the committee Chairman, in collaboration with the Chairman of governors should briefly highlight significant issues and invite comments or questions from other governors. The object is to streamline the work of the board, not to add extra layers to its deliberations. Ultimately, the success of an education committee depends on how effectively it supports, challenges and empowers those who fulfil the school's educational mission. It serves to keep an educational focus at the heart of the business of school governance.

Chapter 12

Some other key committees

a) Marketing and development

Kenneth Edwards

The issue of defining the boundary between the responsibilities of the governors of a school and those of the senior management team can be a source of tension and requires constant review. The board, as the trustees of the charity, has certain legal responsibilities, such as keeping control of the overall finances, complying with employment law and also with health and safety requirements, which governors must accept and cannot devolve to the school managers. That much is not contentious.

What is more debatable is the extent to which the governors are involved in policymaking and its implementation. Of course all schools hope that the relationship between the two is all sweetness and light, but this desirable state is more likely to be achieved – and, if achieved, to be maintained – if the definition of the boundaries is openly discussed between governors and managers, probably on a recurrent basis.

Three facets of the board are important in that respect:

- It has certain inescapable legal responsibilities.
- It should be responsible for deciding the overall strategic direction of the school.
- It is a resource for the school through the expertise and experience of its members.

Tension might arise in the second and third areas. Indeed, there may be interaction between them if the creation of a strategy involves the introduction of activities that are new to the school, and for which there may well be greater expertise among the members of the board than among the school senior managers.

Marketing

Marketing is just such an activity. League tables have increased the sense of competition between schools, while ever-rising fee levels make families search for what appears to be the best value for the money they are about to spend. Schools will be expected to look hard at how they present themselves and improve their image. However, it is wrong to think that marketing is just about attractive brochures or well-run open days aimed at selling the existing product more effectively. It is also about the design of the product and the desires of the market and how best the school can match these.

A question such as 'Should the school aim to expand in order to be able to cover a wider range of both curriculum and extracurricular activities, and will the demand be large enough to justify this enlargement?' is obviously of strategic importance. But the decision will depend on answering a number of specific questions. What is the prediction of likely demand? What extensions to the curriculum are envisaged and will these be attractive? What other extracurricular activities can be provided and how will they influence recruitment? And these all have marketing aspects.

While some elements – such as the potential for further curricular or extracurricular activities – can be answered from within the school, others require marketing information that the school may not have – in fact is unlikely to have. It is possible that the board will have some marketing expertise among its members and if so this will be invaluable. Even if that is the case, it is unlikely that an unpaid board member will have the time to do the necessary work of assessing likely demographic changes in the catchment area, potential competition, and so on. To do this will require appropriate professional expertise that could be provided either by commissioning consultants or by direct employment of a marketing manager.

In the initial stage consultants will almost certainly be necessary in helping to define the role for an employed marketing manager. But perhaps even more important than that will be the need to conduct thorough market research on such topics as likely demographic and economic changes in the catchment area; existence and strength of competitor schools, and developments in education policy concerning local factors or certain types of school. Undertaking this type of research requires specialist skills that consultants (carefully selected of course) can provide. Even with a marketing officer in post it is unlikely that a school will be able to (or would wish to) provide sufficient resources to be able to continue to undertake necessary market research without using consultants for that purpose.

Either way the governors must ensure that such professional expertise is available and that the school does not try to muddle through in an amateur way. Doing this can create tension if the Head and the senior management team try to suggest that marketing can be done by adding the task to the job description of a somewhat under-employed, long-serving staff member. Even at the risk of seeming to tread on to the territory of internal management issues a board must take its overall responsibility for the success of the school as having precedence. If a marketing manager is appointed, this is not the end of the board's responsibilities – for the reports made by the individual will provide information and analysis essential for the board in determining future strategy.

This leads to the conclusion that the marketing manager, while reporting on day-to-day matters to the Head and bursar, should have a work programme determined by a sub-committee of the board, with strong representation from the senior staff, to ensure that the board is supplied with information appropriate to its strategy development role. Furthermore, if the board membership includes one or more individuals with marketing experience, these individuals should be encouraged to have informal contacts with the marketing manager to advise and guide him or her – so fulfilling my third area of board responsibility: acting as a resource.

Marketing is an area relatively new to many schools and there is great variety in the ways in which schools are responding to this challenge. Because of its novelty, governors have a responsibility to ensure that the arrangements put in place are functional and efficient, and that the operation provides a supply of information and analysis that will help both the board to carry out its strategic responsibilities and the school to recruit successfully. If the school management takes the initiative and brings proposals to the board, the board can respond as it thinks appropriate, while always scrutinising the proposals in the light of the responsibilities I have outlined. But the board must also be prepared to take the initiative if necessary!

Development

Many of the same issues arise with development programmes, and with what is the unspoken implication of 'development', namely fundraising. In fact one of the first things a board needs to do is to distinguish between the use of the word 'development' used in the context of long-term planning and strategic development, and the sense in which it is a euphemism for raising money. The former should be considered in the light of the aims and ambitions of the school, initially paying no regard to funding issues. Of course the availability of finance will determine whether any particular ambition is feasible, but money should not decide the overall strategic aims. This stage is clearly a responsibility of the board. The other sense in which development is used then comes into play, as part of a process of generating finance to implement strategic development. This should be *part* of the process, for there may be potential for raising funds by commercial borrowing against a planned growth in fee income if the plans involve expansion: again, a board responsibility.

Turning to the fundraising aspect of development, how should a board be involved? If there is no existing fundraising or if such activity is very new, then it should be seen as a strategic issue to requiring consideration by the governors. A decision to set up a development office must be approved by a board: the funding for it is clearly a financial decision in which governors must be involved, as they should also be in setting targets for the activity. All these aspects are part of the financial and strategic responsibilities of the board. In fact, as with marketing, a board may wish to initiate a fundraising activity if none exists.

Once a development office is up and running, what should be the involvement of the board? Here too there are parallels with the running of a marketing office. Initially the setting up of a development office will need access to relevant expertise that may be present to some extent among the board members, although it is unlikely that this will exist in a form relevant to school situations. It is also unlikely that the senior management of the school will be a source of such expertise.

So it is very probable that a consultant will need to be hired, and this immediately raises the question of who manages the consultant: the board, or the Head and bursar? The answer in my view is to involve both by setting up a sub-committee of the board involving board members who have some knowledge and experience in the area, as well as the Head and bursar and other appropriate staff members. While that arrangement is crucial during the setting up and establishment of a development office, it may well evolve into a regular management committee for the office, again paralleling the arrangements I have suggested for the marketing office. It might be desirable for the Chairman of the board initially to chair such subcommittees – but the important fact is to find amongst board members a chairman who will give the process of establishment some impetus.

Development is necessarily a long-term commitment and successful fundraising depends on building good relationships with potential donors, whether these are alumni or individuals who have an interest in the school. Interest must be converted to commitment and this takes time. Since individual Heads, bursars, development directors and board members come and go, the board collectively must accept the need for a long-term view and maintaining a commitment and a long-term strategy for development. One way in which this can be achieved is through appropriate succession planning for membership of the board by trying to ensure that at any one time there is always at least one member willing to be personally involved in the development activity.

Above all the effectiveness of the relationship between the board and the senior management (particularly the Head and bursar) will depend on individual circumstances, and especially on the personalities involved. In all cases a sense of trust is essential – but this does not mean that each side trusts the other to the extent of drawing a clear line of demarcation and then ignoring each other. Of course the board should entrust the routine day-to-day management of the school to the senior managers, while monitoring this operation – for they do have the ultimate responsibility for the proper running of the school. But there will be issues in which they must be involved in initiating and changing policy – as in setting up a marketing or development office. Thereafter they can ensure that their experience and expertise are used through formal mechanisms, such as sub-committees, and also, importantly, through informal contacts.

b) Remuneration

Alan Weeds

The largest item in the budgets of all schools is staff salaries. Governors set salary levels in independent schools, and remuneration of the most senior staff is best considered by a subcommittee: the remuneration (or senior staff salaries) committee. This reports to the board on salaries and additional benefits such as medical insurance, special arrangements relating to pensions, death-in-service or long-term illness and housing. The tax implications of all benefits have to be a very important factor in these considerations.

The committee will normally meet annually to review salaries, but additional meetings may be arranged at the request of the Head or the board. In the model I am familiar with, the committee has three members: the Chairman and Vice Chairman of governors and the chairman of the finance and general purposes committee. The committee will appoint its own chairman. In view of the need for the committee to be seen to demonstrate its independence to the staff and the sensitivity of senior staff to their salary levels, the committee might choose as chairman a governor distinct from the Chairman of the board, in recognition of the fact that the Head and the board Chairman need to work closely together.

The staff whose remuneration is set by the committee will include the senior management teams of schools within the foundation (senior, preparatory and pre-preparatory schools), comprising the Heads of these schools, deputy heads and others with high levels of overall responsibility (*eg* directors of studies). Non-teaching staff members will include the bursar and deputy bursars (chief finance officers, chief operations officers), the development director and director of marketing (if different from the development director). These senior staff salaries generally do not appear in the school's published documentation.

Factors relating to pay structure and individual emoluments

In setting salary levels, the committee will be aware of national scales in the maintained sector, but greater account will be taken of salaries in comparable independent schools. The reputation of any school is most visibly apparent in its success in achieving the highest grades in GCSE and A level examinations and from the ability of sixth formers to get into universities of their choice. Never has the latter been more competitive. Thus it is of paramount importance to governors that the school can recruit and retain outstanding senior staff that set the standards and implement the vision of the school. The appointment of the Head is probably the most important task for any board, with that of the bursar not very far behind. Schools are large financial institutions for which the bursar carries enormous responsibility: a vibrant school environment and new facilities can be provided only if balance sheets are robust and good financial management is in place. Salaries of the Head and bursar will reflect their overall responsibility for managing every aspect of the school.

As the major cost in school budgets, all salary settlements must be seen in the context of the overall financial position and competing demands for expenditure. The board must also consider this in relation to fee levels and affordability to parents. After a long period when fees have risen at a rate faster than that of average earnings, there is increasing pressure in the current economic climate to restrain fee rises; from 2012, with parents facing much larger university costs, this pressure will inevitably escalate. Few schools have sufficient endowments to fund generous bursaries, but all will want to admit the most talented pupils, irrespective of parental means. Providing even a few bursaries out of fee income places considerable strain on budgets. While wishing to reward staff generously, governors will require clear evidence that higher salaries are fully justified by performance. In order to meet their responsibility to safeguard the charity's assets through careful financial control, it is imperative that governors determine the number of teaching staff appointed, having considered the view of the Head and senior colleagues.

The annual salary review

The committee must have available to it established principles for deciding relativities between different staff, *eg* between Heads of the junior schools as compared to deputy heads in the senior school and between teaching and non-teaching staff. These principles will have been agreed beforehand.

In preparation for the meeting, the Head, in conjunction with the bursar, will circulate as much relevant information as possible about salary levels in comparable schools and details of performance and responsibilities of individual staff with specific recommendations for future pay. Additionally the Head will provide information about his/her and the bursar's salaries and highlight special achievements and major changes of responsibility through the year. AGBIS and the other professional associations produce periodic surveys of salary levels for senior personnel. As the surveys are historic, anonymous and aggregated, the committee may well wish to take these, and the trends they demonstrate, into account.

The Head and bursar will be present for the first part of the meeting to justify their salary recommendations for all staff except themselves, which the committee will discuss with them. The Head and bursar withdraw when the committee discusses their salaries. All decisions will be confirmed in writing to the Head and bursar by the Chairman.

It is likely that defined increments or guaranteed minimum rises for a limited period will be included in the contracts of all newly appointed senior staff. Their purpose is to reward experience and provide incentives, but after this initial period of perhaps five years, percentage rises above any norm set for other staff must be justified on the basis of individual merit. Most staff will be subject to regular external reviews, reports of which will provide important additional information.

Outstanding performance in any given year could be recognised by the use of bonus payments, which can provide very generous one-off rewards for achievement. This is generally not popular with staff because bonuses are neither consolidated nor pensionable. Nevertheless, bonuses can be an effective means of rewarding additional responsibilities, such as standing in for relatively short periods (less than a year) when more senior staff are given leave. It is possible that pension rule changes in the future might severely restrict pensionable pay rises, which may make bonus payments more acceptable.

Other issues

First of all, comparability issues can be very contentious and decisions of the committee may not always be readily accepted. For this reason, although the primary conduit to the committee is via the Head, occasions may arise when aggrieved individuals pressurise the Head. In these situations, and subject to the agreement of the Head, I favour allowing individuals to make their case directly to the committee or one of its members, either in writing or through a personal hearing. Recommendations by the committee in such cases would be discussed with the Head prior to any decision being passed to the individual. This has two advantages: first, all members of staff know they may have to justify their case to an independent committee; secondly, by transferring the responsibility directly to the committee, it protects the Head from any accusation that cases were not pressed sufficiently strongly.

Comparability between teaching and non-teaching staff can also be contentious, but here the external market provides a yardstick. Outstanding development directors and bursars are in short supply, and their skills have to be rewarded appropriately. Every effort should be made to demonstrate that rewards are fair, because it is essential that senior management work together as a team to the benefit of all in the school.

Secondly, special issues may arise in the lead-up to retirement. Governors may wish to enhance salaries of senior staff nearing retirement either as a reward for service given or sometimes as a means to ensure that retirement occurs at the most advantageous time for the school's future plans. The abolition of the current fixed retirement age is likely to make the latter a general issue for governors in relation to many members of staff. At the same time, there is increasing concern about the long-term unaffordability of the current unfunded public sector pension scheme resulting from increasing longevity and demographic changes. Major changes to the scheme will be needed to reduce the costs to future generations of contributors and taxpayers.

At the time of writing annual pensionable pay rises allowed by the Teachers' Pension (TP) Scheme (currently a final salary scheme) are restricted to 10% in the final three years, but this may change. Whether or not it remains so, the scheme's arrangements are not intended by the Department for Education as a general invitation to enhance pensions. The board must exercise this flexibility responsibly, being aware of the danger of setting precedents for other staff and in the light of the fact that independent schools participate in the TP scheme on a concessionary basis and not by right. Changes recommended by the committee must be justified on the basis of personal merit and only in the most exceptional circumstances for other reasons.

In summary, the committee has a very important role in setting remuneration and benefit levels in order to provide strong incentives and to reward personal achievement, while recognising the need for transparency and fairness in relation to other salaries and the constraints imposed by budgetary needs. The independence of the committee should provide protection for the Head against undue pressure and ensure that the board is satisfied that remuneration levels can at all times be justified.

Chapter 13

Policies, complaints and appeals

Nigel Richardson

It is often said that we live in a highly litigious age. All sorts of complex reasons are advanced for this, from human rights legislation (blame the EU) to the rise of ambulance-chasing lawyers (blame the USA). Some see it in political terms: the electorate, encouraged by patients' charters, is less inclined to accept top-down government or excuses for its failure. People have thus become more inclined to complain – about the perceived failures of the local hospital; poor service in a restaurant or too many cones on the motorway. Others say that this all stems from a change in basic human attitudes: we are more stressed-out by the pressures of daily life; less satisfied; more aggressive; more preoccupied than in the past with individual rights rather than with duties.

Whatever the reasons, independent schools cannot be immune from these trends, and the complaining culture that comes with them: schools provide a service and they charge a fee for doing so. Moreover, life being essentially unfair, no school, however customer-savvy, can inoculate itself against the risks of being complained against. The difference between the best schools and the worst is that the best ones attract fewer complaints and deal with them better, thus making people less likely to complain.

Even if schools cannot protect themselves against all complaints, they can minimise their impact. When complaints arise, they should be dealt with in a way most likely to assuage hurt feelings, and to prevent the complaint spiralling to a level of intensity out of all proportion to the original issue. Above all, schools should *be prepared*.

So how can a governing body contribute to a state of preparedness? As with so many of the issues described in this book, it should not attempt to micro-manage, but it should assure itself that the management has put sound procedures in place to minimise the risk that complaints will arise, and to minimise the damage if they prove to be intractable.

This consists of actions at several levels. Firstly, when times are good and the school is running smoothly, by following one of the most basic rules of good PR: seeking to establish a reputation for sound procedures, good communication and a reasonable, common sense approach in all things. The board should encourage the management to explain carefully to parents the reasons for such potentially contentious decisions as a change of exam syllabus or a new school uniform. Then it should also practise what it preaches; the Chairman's announcement of a fee rise should take pains to regret that it is necessary; if possible to state that it is the lowest for some years, and to describe the reasons for it (higher energy charges; increased employers' pension contributions *etc*), rather than merely proclaiming it in a two-line 'take it or leave it' letter to hard-pressed parents.

Then, when the waters become more choppy (as they inevitably will, at times, in any organisation with a large number of employees and essentially unpredictable young people), parents and others are more likely to see you in a positive light; to give you more of the benefit of the doubt than they would otherwise have done, and less likely to seek legal redress in the wake of disappointing public exam results.

Secondly, governors should ensure that there are proper measures in place for drawing up and reviewing the most relevant documentation. This will require the Head and bursar/clerk to work closely with the school's legal advisers.

Broadly speaking, these documents fall in to three categories:

- Those concerned with the employment of **staff**: contracts; grievance and disciplinary procedures; appeals against dismissal; intellectual property *etc.*
- Those relating to how the school conducts its business with **parents**: admissions procedures; general contractual matters, terms and conditions; fees policy. The terms and conditions should include a clear statement about the circumstances in which the school may demand fees in lieu of notice after the withdrawal of a pupil.

• Those relating to its dealings with **pupils**: policies on such matters as behaviour, discipline and sanctions; child protection; confidentiality and references; day-to-day supervision, including welfare, medical and pastoral provision.

The governing body is likely to delegate the drawing-up of many or all of these documents to the management, but it cannot evade legal responsibility for the annual formal approval of, for example, the child protection policy. It should ensure that the Head and bursar compile a programme of rolling reviews, and that they are aware of which of the key policies need to be presented for approval at each board meeting. A board can avoid the huge proliferation of paper by sending material electronically to governors (either via a PDF or through a secure/ dedicated section of the school website), and the Chairman should insist that wherever possible queries to the management about the drafts should be raised *ahead* of the meeting, rather than governors unpicking them during the meeting itself. Board members *en masse* do not write good policies, and they can waste a great deal of time trying to do so.

All schools are required to have a clearly-stated policy on the handling of concerns and complaints, and how they are to be made. This must be made available to parents. There must be a reference in the prospectus or similar publication to the means by which the Chairman of governors may be contacted (perhaps by post, c/o the clerk). The handbook of the Independent Schools' Inspectorate (ISI) lays out the key requirements. Different legal firms will draw up slightly different policies, but most are based on a staged procedure along these lines:

• Stage 1 will normally state the school's hope that most concerns can be resolved informally, and will include a list of which members of staff to consult about which type of concern (curriculum, pastoral, staff *etc*). It should state how rapidly the school will aim to respond. Some policies divide this stage into two distinct levels; complaints to a teacher, form tutor, housemaster or section head, and those that then have to be referred upwards – but still informally – to senior management.

- Stage 2 is likely to involve the complainant filling in a standard form and providing documentation to the Head or deputy. Again it should give a likely response time, and may include the provision for the Head to ask a senior member of staff and/or a governor to act as 'investigator'.

- Stage 3 – for those still not satisfied after the earlier stages – involves a formal complaint addressed to the Chairman of governors. S/he will then arrange an investigation similar in form to that laid down in stage 2.

- Stage 4 – if all else has failed – involves a formally constituted complaints panel, comprising school governors *and at least one member who is independent of the governance and management of the school.* The policy should set out the procedures and broad timings to be followed; how evidence will be taken and assessed; how a decision will be arrived at and conveyed to all parties and, ultimately, how an unsatisfied complainant can make representations to the ISI (or, in some circumstances involving very young children, Ofsted). It might also include whether or not the governors are prepared to allow legal representation by either side.

It all sounds highly complex and bureaucratic, and in some situations, it can become so. However, there are now plenty of legal firms specialising in the compilation of such policies (bursars and others do not have to reinvent the wheel), and once compiled the annual review is normally a comparatively simple task. Schools that are efficient and well thought-of are more likely to be able to avoid concerns reaching Stages 2, 3 or 4.

The governing body is most likely to become actively involved in cases where the stakes are highest – *ie* when the Head has decided to expel or require the removal of a pupil. Appeals or review hearings are increasingly inevitable in a society in which employment and school records, character references and child protection registers have become so significant, and in which exam success and university entry have become such high-stakes matters.

Formal review hearings (conducted in accordance with a separate policy) require the involvement of governors. Some useful advice:

1) Remember at all times that a review hearing is quite distinct from a legal process – even though one or more lawyers may possibly be involved, either as supporters for one side (see above) or as panel members (see below).

2) It is best for all governing bodies to assume that they will need to set up an appeal hearing sooner or later. Unlike a complaints procedure or employee dismissal procedure, there is no actual requirement for at least one independent member to sit on a review panel but, at times, this may be hard to dispute on the grounds of natural justice. Many parents or their lawyers will dispute the composition of a panel where, for example, a retired governor or retired local Head is drafted in as the independent voice: such people are, understandably, seen as non-neutral. It is therefore sensible to identify *well ahead of any problem appearing* a few people with the ability, impartiality and time to give to this role, and to get their agreement in principle to serve.

   It is also possible to take on a lawyer in this role, but the benefits in terms of expertise have to be weighed against the risk of the parents questioning their independence if the school is paying their fees.

3) A Chairman (or any other governor) who has been consulted by the Head during the earlier stages of a serious disciplinary matter is also deemed to be non-neutral, and thus ineligible to take part in any review hearing. Thus, at the first sign of a possible dismissal or expulsion, a wise Head should ask the Chairman: "Do you want me to involve you in this, or should I talk to the Vice Chairman, and enable you to keep your later options open?"

4) It is inevitable that both sides in such situations will feel hurt and/ or anxious – possibly aggressive.

   For the employee subject to dismissal, a future career may be at stake. For the parent or pupil, premature departure from the school, perhaps after many years of fee-paying and (for example, in the case of extreme bullying) possibly with an unblemished record up to this point, may be a significant long-term setback.

Don't forget, either, the high stakes for the Head: if the governors find against the Head, his/her authority will have suffered a very significant and very public rebuff (and it will certainly be felt as such). Even the calmest and most experienced Head, utterly confident about the sanctions meted out, can become distinctly stressed by having to go through an appeal or review process: it may well happen only very rarely; the Head is essentially unused to having his/her authority questioned in this way, and s/he may actually very much like the pupil concerned

5) Thus the choice of the appeal-hearing chairman is a crucial one. The role needs to be taken on by someone capable of assessing quite complex evidence, dealing with everyone sensitively while keeping cool but firm in the face of any undue pressure.

6) Even if the review panel eventually upholds the school's position, if the review has been well-conducted it can play an important part in reconciliation and bringing closure to the employee or parent.

7) Unless the circumstances of the case make it quite inappropriate, such closure can also be brought about at least in part if the school feels able to offer some help to ease the situation: it should never be unnecessarily unhelpful or obstructive.

Where a pupil below the age of 18 who has been required to leave needs to remain in full time education, it is quite normal for a Head to offer to speak supportively but honestly to his/her opposite number in a prospective new school – although it is tactically sensible for the parent to make the initial approach, and to be completely up-front about the situation from the outset.

If a pupil's preparation for imminent public exams has been put seriously at risk, are relevant subject teachers prepared to offer discreet private tuition out of school? Can the pupil be allowed to return to the school under strictly controlled conditions to sit these exams? (It is not always easy for a candidate to find a suitable exam centre at short notice.) Can the Head write in support of a university reference later on?

8) *Before* the matter is heard or resolved, consider whether there will be any rapid PR measures to be taken – whichever way the verdict goes.

Most of these principles will also apply when a member of staff appeals against significant disciplinary action or dismissal. In complex employment hearings, some schools have used an outside figure with legal expertise as Chairman, partly to lessen the risk of exposure to an employment tribunal later on – but this inevitably comes at high cost.

In all these scenarios, one returns to the same old maxim: *Be Prepared.* It always pays in the long run.

I am very grateful to John Deakin, a partner in the pastoral team at Veale Wasbrough Vizards, for his advice during the preparation of this chapter.

Chapter 14

The importance of development planning

Ian Power

There comes a time in the affairs of most Heads and governors when there is a need for what might be best termed a 'Baldrick moment'. For those unfamiliar with the eponymous character from the *Blackadder* series, Baldrick, described by his master, Captain Blackadder, as having 'the intellectual capacity of a dirty potato', has a 'cunning plan'. On hearing this shocking and unexpected announcement, Blackadder asks: "Is it as cunning as a fox that has just been made Professor of Cunning at Oxford University?"

What would any Head give for a plan of such guile and cunning; what would any chair of governors give for a plan so devastating in its simplicity that it could end forever that sinking feeling generated by what might euphemistically be called, 'the fear of small numbers', whether they be pupils or figures on the bottom line?

Whether it is a cunning plan to escape the perils of the First World War, or one that will ensure the future success of the school, we all need one. And a proper, well-articulated school development plan is just that: a means to ensure the future success of the school, or at least the foreseeable part, anyway. But what characterises the future success of the school and how can this be encapsulated in a plan that is guaranteed to deliver such success?

The answer to this question takes us to the heart of development planning. Such planning starts even before a new Head takes up post. Many will remember the immortal words uttered by either an optimistic or unsuspecting Chairman of governors at the final interview stage: "If you were successful in gaining this appointment, what would be your vision for the school?" The eager candidates rush to fill the inevitable silence that follows with generalisations about criteria for success; the wonders of the school (and the governors, of course), and how greatness is only just around the corner – assuming, equally naturally, that they appoint the right candidate! However, on more careful and measured analysis the fine words pale, as they should, and the successful candidate is judged, not on the depth of the argument, but simply on its strength and plausibility. No: real vision and the subsequent development planning come later, far removed from the rarefied atmosphere of the interview room.

So where should Heads, whether new in post or at a key point in headship, start the planning process with their governing body? Does it all begin with a vision: a thunderbolt from heaven; even a Damascus moment – or is it something deeper and more prolonged? Surely it is the latter, but the questions still remain: how long and how deep?

There is plenty of advice available on development planning. A quick search of the internet reveals a plethora of 'off the shelf packages' that sadly seem aimed more at satisfying the requirements of inspection (especially Ofsted's requirements), than seriously challenging the school and its management to seek real improvement. Good sense suggests that such packages are best avoided unless, of course, your only concern really is to keep the inspectors at bay. Assuming that a desire to seek real and sustained school improvement is the basis for future planning, there might just be a few other things worthy of consideration. Perhaps the obvious place to start is with a simple set of questions:

- What is the vision for the school?
- Who shares this vision, and who articulates the plan?
- What are the success criteria?
- When do we expect to know when we have achieved such success?

What is the vision for the school?

I can think of a number of new Heads who have been told by their governing bodies to produce a paper 'summarising their vision for the school', on the assumption, one presumes, that it is simply that: the

Head's vision for the school. Governors, and Heads, need to be wary of such elephant traps.

No doubt the Head, as chief executive, will have identified areas of concern; underachievement; even outright failure, in his or her initial analysis of the school and its performance. However, it would be a brave Head who wrote such a document in isolation, based on perhaps only three to six months of observation and intermittent thought. No: a true vision for the school can only stem from what might best be termed 'forensic evaluation'. Such evaluation goes beyond simple self-evaluation (which can run the risk of becoming a glorified form of navel-gazing) and instead seeks out systematic evidence regarding the performance of the school, and just as importantly, the views of its various constituencies: governors, parents, staff and pupils.

Once you have a sense of the 'vision', of course, it does not stop there: you need a plan to deliver the vision – and who better placed to write this plan than the Head? Beware the Chairman of governors who suggests idly: "Headmaster, we need a development plan. Perhaps you could put something together over the summer holiday?" Visions come to mind of a hassled Head throwing together a plan on a beach in the south of France, surrounded by screaming children and frustrated partner. This is neither the time nor the place for vision and development planning.

So where should the hassled Head start? Vision must begin with what the school actually is, and what it suggests it stands for – so what better place to start than in the founding document or the earliest prospectus? Such research is always worthwhile as it enables the Head to link his or her vision with the past: something that is vital for all concerned with the school, whatever their status or role. Put another way: before you can plan the journey you need to know both where you are and where you have come from.

Such documents inevitably focus on values, and it is these values that should underpin the vision. What is more, a vision based on values is much more likely than other grand statements to resonate with the various constituencies that represent the school community, and in addition provide the much-needed anchor in uncertain times.

Hopefully, your vision will have something to do with education (which should not come as a surprise!) and resources. It will probably not go much beyond such broad statements of intent; nor should it. It is the *next* stage – evidenced-based development planning – that takes the vision; converts it into something more tangible, and to a certain degree, more measurable. But who should be involved: the Head; the governors; the staff; the parents; the pupils?

Who shares this vision, and who articulates the plan?

Development planning is not the preserve of the single-minded, hero-Head, setting out on the long, lonely road to glory. Nor is it the place for a governing body to decide what sort of school it wants and simply to instruct the Head to deliver it. Development planning has to be research-led, and collaborative both in formation and delivery. Experience suggests that even long-standing governors and governing bodies can be unclear as to the next steps in the future development of the school. They, like a new Head, need intelligence and information and what better way to do this than to survey systematically the key constituencies of the school? Such carefully thought out research and analysis will form the basis of the plan, linking closely with a vision based on values and education, and ensuring that the whole school community understands the thinking behind it (even if its members do not all necessarily agree with the outcome).

What are the success criteria?

Schools are complex organisations: organic in structure, with a plethora of connections and inter-connections that make systematic development difficult to devise and implement. A development plan has to be sufficiently flexible to take account of this complexity, and needs to have the capacity to be rapidly overtaken by external events. By way of example, consider a coeducational boarding and day school where boarding numbers have fallen steadily over the past ten years. The development plan might suggest ways to maintain, or even increase, boarding numbers (recruitment overseas, or a more flexible approach). However, the collapse of boarder recruitment at 11 or 13, for no obvious reason, could change this approach dramatically – tipping the balance between what was once seen as a boarding school with day pupils into a day school with notional boarding.

In this regard success criteria should be as much about the *process* as they are about the *outcome*. Governors and Heads, in leading their schools, are usually in a good position to control the processes, but the outcomes can often be at the mercy of seemingly fickle events outside their control. In the past, such uncertainty has caused some to shy away from detailed development planning, but surely this misses the point? Effective development planning is about understanding the school: where it is and where it might be in the future; it is about engaging with all of its constituencies, and in so doing, creating a lasting dialogue.

To reiterate: it is the processes of planning that are important, not the outcomes. Put another way: after a suitable period of time it might well be possible to 'tick off' certain achievements (higher academic standards; the opening of the new performing arts centre) but there will also be failures as well (boarding numbers have fallen). The importance and significance lie not with these failures of *outcome*, but with the successes of *process*. A governing body might have little influence over a downturn in the economy, but it can establish through its chief executive an effective dialogue with its stakeholders and, in so doing, remain responsive to events and still in control of its own destiny.

When do we expect to know when we have achieved success?

The astute reader has probably already discovered the answer to this final question. Success might well be identified in terms of 'easy goals': results; new examination systems; new buildings; even greater pupil numbers – but the greater success comes from the process of planning and delivery, and in the engagement of the whole school community. Off-the-shelf development plans rarely acknowledge the greater importance of the process and the dialogue, focusing instead on the outcomes and the measurable success criteria. Sustainable development planning is organic by nature: flexible and responsive. It cannot guarantee success, but it will enable a school and its wider community to put in place responsive systems and processes that should enable it to respond to the challenges, and to create and nurture the climate that engages all in the highest-quality education.

Those who have worked in senior positions in education know that the realisation of a vision, and the underpinning development planning, are not easy. However, being prepared to gather information, views and evidence in a systematic way is the cornerstone of success, and the basis for that panacea of the truly 'cunning plan'. As Captain Blackadder would say: "I have a plan so cunning you could put a tail on it and call it a weasel."

Chapter 15

Delivering the plan: project management

Alan Browne

"So, Chairman, we have agreed where we want the school to be in three years time, but how are we going to get there?" "It is a wonderful vision, but can we really afford it?" "How long is all this going to take?"

It will not be long after a school has completed the demanding task of agreeing a plan or vision for the future and the Chairman of the governors has obtained the governing body's agreement to it, that several members of the board will ask these questions, or some very like them. It is right that they should. The exciting envisioning process now gives way to the more mundane, but still very important, process of delivery.

The nature of the plan or vision will vary from the straightforward, such as deciding to demolish an old gymnasium and replace it with a modern sports hall, to the very complex, such as deciding to merge with another school; move all teaching to one of the sites (which in turn needs substantial extension); dispose of the other site, and reduce pupil and teacher numbers by 20%. And there are an almost infinite number of other plans and visions that might be decided upon.

Although the number of possible plans and visions that schools pursue is large, and their nature diverse, they have sufficient features in common for the same principles to apply to managing them. The rest of this chapter will look at those principles and how they should be applied.

At this stage it will be useful to distinguish between two different types of management process: project management and programme management. A project usually has a clearly definable deliverable at the end: a new sports hall; the rolling out of a new curriculum; the IB (International Baccalaureate) instead of, or as well as, A levels.

Whatever the nature of the project, it requires careful management if it is to deliver what is wanted; at the time that it is wanted; for a price that can be afforded. A programme usually has an outcome that it is required to deliver: a school that has 50% more pupils or a merger with another school, perhaps. It will usually require the execution of a number of projects in an optimum sequence to deliver the required outcome of the programme as a whole. Each of those constituent projects will need managing, but the overall programme, of which they are part, also needs managing. Thus management at two levels is required – programme level and project level – rather than just one. Moreover it is likely that different individuals or bodies will provide the management at the two levels.

The brief

At the outset those who are to deliver the project need to be given a clear brief, to ensure that what is delivered matches what is required. At this level of principles, it doesn't matter whether the project is to be managed by a school employee or an external party hired in for the purpose. They need a brief. The brief will describe in detail what is to be delivered. If it is a sports hall, the brief will indicate the required size; the activities it must accommodate; and perhaps the delivery date and the available budget. The brief is received by the person charged with the delivery of the project, who we shall now call the project manager (PM).

At the outset, the brief may be short and simple, but may evolve as the project proceeds. The PM should ensure that the brief is clear enough to enable the project to proceed, and at an early stage should check how long it will take to deliver, and how much it will cost. Having ascertained good initial estimates of cost and time, approval should be sought, but from whom? This leads us on to the next topic: governance.

Governance

The Head, and particularly the bursar, will be carrying out smaller projects on a continuous basis: training, maintenance, building upgrades *etc*. For these items a well-established approval and authority regime will exist, and governance probably just happens.

However for a larger project or programme of work, which could have major implications for the whole school, a clearly defined and specific system of governance needs to be put in place.

In such circumstances three roles need to be filled in the governance system:

1. The project board: ultimate responsibility normally rests with the whole governing body, but it may be appropriate to appoint a sub-committee of three or four governors who will meet more frequently to monitor the project and deal with the decisions that the project requires. Such a sub-committee should ideally have substantial delegated authority.

2. A project champion: this role should normally be taken by a governor, but it might be carried out by the Head or bursar. Many different names are used, but the role is that of the senior person who takes overall responsibility for the delivery of the project. If it is a governor, s/he will be on, and will usually chair, any project sub-committee of the board. The project champion is the mentor for the project leader.

3. The project leader: this person takes the day to day responsibility for the delivery of the project and acts as the client for all those carrying out activities that contribute to the delivery of the project, providing decisions and approvals as required, and referring them upwards as necessary. The project leader is often the bursar, but may be the Head, a deputy head or a deputy bursar. S/he should definitely be a school employee.

The responsibilities of each of these three bodies or individuals should be clearly recorded and the details circulated to all parties including the project manager.

Planning

At the outset, a project or programme needs to be planned. The first thing is to identify all the activities that need to be carried out to achieve the goal. For a building project these will include design; planning permission; tendering and construction. However, they may also include dealing with constraints on the land; listed building permission; traffic planning (if the school is in an area with heavy traffic) and many more. In a major programme it could include amendments to trust deeds; permissions from the charity commissioners and agreements with the Equal Opportunities Commission (if a school is changing from single sex to coeducational). Any type of project could include the need for bank loans or fundraising. The important thing is that *all* the activities required to complete the project are identified and that someone is responsible for the completion of each of them: see the section on work stream management below.

In the inception stages of the project, the aim should be to minimise expenditure, consistent with generating sufficient information to make good decisions. The 80:20 rule should be applied whenever possible: *ie* work to get 80% of the results for 20% of the effort.

If the project involves building work, such work is best done in the context of an overall master plan for the site. Then, as each building is constructed, it fits with what is already there and what is yet to be built. When the master plan is drawn up, and the buildings are to be constructed in stages, it should include details of how the school will operate in the various interim stages *before* everything is built.

Time

Once the activities are known and the precedence identified, a programme can be drawn up showing the total time needed. School projects are usually constrained by the school year. Schools frequently want projects to be completed in time for the beginning of the new school year, but paradoxically it is often best if the project doesn't cause major disruption before the end of an earlier one. Work that can be done in a holiday will have less impact than work done in term time. With decisions taken on how the project work should be fitted into the school year, the project programme can be fitted into calendar time. Remember to allow time contingency, if the completion date is critical.

Cost

With all the activities identified and a programme set, the cost needs to be estimated. The project manager may need help here from cost management professionals and/or contractors/suppliers. As well as the known costs, a contingency should be held for the unknowns. When HM

Treasury considers applications for financial support for PFI (Private Finance Initiative) projects from public sector bodies, it applies an 'optimism bias' factor to the estimated costs, on the basis that those who really want to deliver a project can sometimes allow their enthusiasm and optimism to over-ride caution and prudence. Governing bodies should be satisfied that cost estimates allow for everything known, with a reasonable allowance for the unknown. This aspect is looked at a little more below in the context of managing risk.

Affordability

For a simple maintenance or training project, the cost will be set against the relevant budget and a straightforward decision can be made on whether it can be afforded this year or must wait until next year, or whether another project must be delayed to permit this one. However a really major project: a school move; a merger; a decision to downsize; or a major building project, is likely to be sufficiently big to need a rather more sophisticated approach to be taken to the question of affordability. At the largest end, the project could have a major impact on the school's business plan. It is important to remember that the school *is* a business as well as a school.

Some schools operate on a simple accounting system: as long as income exceeds expenditure this year, and it looks as though the same will be true next year, everyone is content. However, embarking on a major project may mean that a rather more long-term and complex financial business model is required. Even if the school itself doesn't feel it needs such an approach (and it is suggested that such a view would be misguided), it may well be required by any bank that is asked for loan finance, or by a major donor. My local village hall committee had to produce a full 20-year business plan to get an £80,000 grant from the Lottery Board for an upgrade.

The financial business plan should look at the totality of the school's finances, including all income and expenditure, over an extended period. The length of that period will be determined by aspects such as the time to receive all the donations from an appeal, or the planned payback period of a loan. It must also address the fact that things may not turn out as hoped: the money raised by the appeal might be less than expected; a planned increase in pupil numbers might be slower than anticipated; interest rates might increase unexpectedly; a hostile government might change the VAT position on schools. To address these possibilities, a formalised sensitivity analysis should be carried out that looks at the consequence of one or more of these events occurring.

Business case approvals

Once a reasonable estimate has been made of programme and cost, it is usual for the governance system to review the project and give a formal agreement to proceed. However, getting to the point of a good estimate and a viable programme is likely to have incurred significant costs. If the project is large, it is probably wise to give a budget for this initial development work at the outset. This initial budget sanction is often referred to as 'Outline Business Case Approval', and the approval that follows the accurate programme and cost estimate is known as 'Full Business Case Approval'. The titles are unimportant in themselves, but going through these steps gives a good discipline and control of the process and costs.

Risk management

The American Defence Secretary, Donald Rumsfeld, famously drew the distinction between known unknowns and unknown unknowns. The primary aim of risk assessment is to identify the things that might go wrong; to identify those that are most likely and/or would have the greatest impact, and then to manage them. It is not sufficient to decide, like Asterix, that the only thing that frightens you is the possibility of the sky falling in, and then to ignore every other risk.

On larger projects the risk management can be taken a stage further to a quantified risk assessment. This aims to cost the consequence of the risks identified, and by a statistical combination with the quantified likelihood, to calculate the contingency that should be held to deal with the risks.

Managing change

Every project provides the opportunity to improve the school for the benefit of pupils and staff. Consequently it will generate considerable interest and enthusiasm – plus, possibly, jealousy if the result benefits one group or department more than others. Getting to the final brief and detailed plan tends to be an iterative process, as different groups press their interests and lobby accordingly. That is normal, but any change from what is agreed at the outset needs to be controlled in a way appropriate to the stage of the project, with its associated costs and time implications assessed and accepted before it is approved. The aim should be to limit change to the period between outline and full business case approval as far as possible. The project definition, approved with the full business case together with its associated budget and programme, should be the reference point for managing any future change. In a long and complex project a later definition may be substituted as the reference point as the project progresses. To retain proper control, the governors should pay attention to the following points:

- All change should be formally approved by the project leader.
- A change introduced to save money can cause as many problems as one introduced to improve the product.
- Ensure that all stakeholders are consulted about possible changes.
- Once a project is under way (especially a building project), it is often cheaper to let it run or to omit something, and then make the change afterwards.

Public relations and internal relations

A lot of people may be affected by a school's project: pupils; parents; staff; alumni, and neighbours, amongst others. Governors will probably wish to manage carefully any information about the project, especially if there are sensitivities about what is planned: otherwise the rumour mill will do the job for them.

A single individual should be charged with PR and the same or another individual with internal relations. This approach will ensure a consistent message. If there are major sensitivities, consider the appointment of a PR professional. The cost may ensure that announcements are targeted for best effect and drafted to minimise the risk of being misinterpreted. The outcome can be the difference between opposition and support or, at worst, grudging acceptance.

Managing programmes

Everything written so far applies to programmes as much as projects. However, with programmes there is an added level of complexity. The total programme has to be divided up into projects, each with their own brief, budget and timeline. Only once these have been produced, or at least estimated, for each constituent project can the cost and time for the whole programme be estimated. The programme manager needs to ensure that the work is done for each project; that the interfaces are managed, and any conflicts (which may be related to issues of space or time), are resolved. Only then can the total cost and time of the whole programme be estimated and approved. Ideally the programme manager should be a different person from any of the project managers, as this role requires a different approach and perspective from the one exercised by the project managers.

The project and programme manager

So far we have looked at the functions that must be carried out to manage the project, but not at who should take the role. Particular skills, some of which have been identified in the sections above, are needed to manage projects and programmes, and time needs to be set aside for the work that each will involve. It is perfectly possible that one or more existing members of the school staff have the correct skills-set to manage the project or programme. However, if s/he is to take on this role, which is likely to be time consuming, s/he may need to be relieved of other duties. If that is not possible, it will be necessary either to hire in someone, either as a short-term appointment or to employ a firm of specialist consultant project managers.

If an external manager is hired, the school's project leader will probably delegate some, but not all, of his responsibilities to the project manager. There remains a key client leadership function that must be carried out by the client.

Work stream management

In the early stages of the project, all the activities that are needed to deliver the project should have been identified. To deliver the project, each work stream needs to deliver its output at the appropriate time. One of the key jobs of the project manager, rather like the conductor of an orchestra, is to ensure that the leader of each work stream knows what s/he must do, and by when it must be done. S/he must also have identified what s/he needs from other work streams; that they are all holding to programme, and that the necessary support is on hand if problems occur. A non-exhaustive list of work streams for a building project is:

- Design, including architect, structural engineer and building services engineer.
- Cost management: quantity surveyor.
- Specialist consultants, including possibly: planning, traffic, acoustics, fire.
- Educational implications.
- Public relations.
- Internal relations.
- Staff issues: recruitment, redundancy, training.
- Fundraising.
- Loan finance.
- Site acquisition.
- Legal: various including restrictive covenants, trust matters, charity law.
- Construction: building contractor.

Governors need to be satisfied that suitable processes are in place for managing the coordination of *all* the appropriate work streams. The overall aim should be appropriate management. If a small and simple project is over-managed, it may lead to waste of time, additional costs and frustration. However if a major or complex project is *under-managed*, it may lead to major increased cost, loss of reputation or catastrophe.

Appointments

It is likely that the school will have to appoint external consultants to deliver the activity in a number of the work streams. The first priority should be firms or individuals with strong skills and good experience in the relevant area: seek recommendations from other schools and business contacts, and always take up references from their previous clients. Fees may be charged as lump sums, hourly rates or percentages of construction value (especially for building designers and quantity surveyors). The decision on the type of fee structure will depend on how well the scope of work is defined. If it is well defined, a lump sum may be best. If it is less well designed, a time basis may be better – at least, until the scope becomes clearer. It is quite reasonable to change the charging basis part of the way through, by agreement. A particular responsibility of the project manager during the appointment process should be to ensure that there are no gaps between the responsibilities of the various consultants. Perhaps surprisingly, standard forms of appointment do not necessarily ensure that.

Appropriate types of contract for a building contractor are a more complex area. It is suggested that governors seeks specialist advice from a professional building project manager or quantity surveyor, either of whom will be able to advise the pros and cons of the different types of contract for a particular project.

Do we need an external project manager?

Large-scale, external project management is likely to mean that a Head, and even some bursars, start to experience a professional *modus operandi* of which they have little or no previous experience.

Embarking on such an approach has obvious cost implications in itself. Any school considering a medium to large-scale project – whether it be an unusually complex new building, a property acquisition or even a merger with another institution – needs to ask itself some fundamental questions:

- Can a school afford such external support?
- Can it *not* afford it, given
    i) the expertise required;
    ii) the potential pitfalls that it might encounter in delivering ambitious plans;
    iii) the need to get all the constituent parts and interested parties working together; all making their contributions at the right time and in the right order;
    iv) the demands that may fall on the already hard-pressed management?

In such circumstances – or even when first considering the pros and cons of any big initiative – it may be worth commissioning what might be called a 'quick and dirty' study of the proposed project: an outline assessment of the various demands and work streams that such an initiative may require in order to bring it to successful realisation. Such a report – which might run to 15-20 sides of A4, based on one or two initial visits – should cost little more than a proportion of a single pupil fee – yet it might save a great deal of angst and money in the long run by giving a clear picture of what will be required at the outset.

How to be a bad client

Since this book is for governors, it seems appropriate to finish the chapter with a look at the role of the client in the delivery of the project. It is often assumed that the project manager's biggest headaches are wilful architects; overpaid and under-performing consultants and contractors; and suppliers running late and claiming large amounts of extra money. Some or all of these headaches may indeed be the biggest. But regrettably it is sometimes the *client* who causes the greatest problems.

For those clients who are determined to make the project manager and team *really* earn their salaries or fees, here are some (tongue in cheek) key pointers:

- Drive the fees of the project manager and other professionals down so low that they cannot do a proper job.
- Issue an ill-considered and incomplete brief at the outset.
- Change your mind about what you want as often as possible. The team will enjoy running a sweepstake on what you are going to change next.
- Have at least three members of the school body giving instructions to the team, which are ideally conflicting.
- Insist on the team delivering all their reports and output exactly on time and then take at least four times as long as planned to give approvals or decisions, insisting that the team makes up the lost time in the next stage.
- Never let the project manager into the school's decision-making process to avoid the risk of practicality impacting on this week's dream.
- Always make sure there is a blame culture. It lends such a good atmosphere to the project and brings out the best in everyone working on it.

Chapter 16

Finding a new Head

Nearly all schools conduct the selection process for a new Head and other senior personnel in one of three ways. Most will place a public advertisement; some will use in addition either a self-employed adviser from within the independent school sector or a headhunting company that searches for candidates for posts in a wide variety of walks of life. In this chapter two former Heads, each with experience of one of these methods, discuss their experiences.

a) The role of the adviser

Hugh Monro

The appointment of a new Head is far and away the most important role of any governing body. Most governors are involved in the process only once or twice in their term of office, so they need all the support and advice that they can get.

So where to start? Before anything else, it is important to establish three main guiding documents. These are a person specification, the job description, and a timeline. Decisive and strong leadership from the Chairman is needed to establish how these will be decided and also the way in which the whole process will be managed. This usually involves the creation of an appointment committee from within the board, which will be responsible for the process, right the way through to the final round of interviews. Who should be in this group? The Chairman and four or five others, who represent a genuine cross-section of the board, should be a starting point.

Most boards now involve the help of someone from outside their own ranks in the process. Several options are available. Well established, national and international headhunting firms can offer experience and excellence guidance. They usually have sensible templates for the process and can have knowledge of suitable candidates; however, sometimes they can have several appointments running simultaneously. There have been occasions when they have misjudged the needs of the school and produced a long list which contains only two or three genuine candidates and many 'serial applicants'.

An alternative is to use a recently retired Head as an adviser. This has the advantage of having someone who has recent experience of running a school and useful, relevant contacts; on the other hand, there may not be a high degree of the all-important administrative backup and organisation. Much may depend on how efficient and confidential the school's bursar or clerk to the governors can be, and how much the school is prepared to administer the process 'in house'.

Setting the process in motion

The creation of the 'person spec' should allow for contributions from governors, staff and others. A list of both essential and desirable qualifications, experience, achievements and interests needs to be agreed. This is best done by a small group of governors. A sensible timetable for advertising, the closing date and the rounds of interviews should be clearly set out. The *Times Educational Supplement* (*TES*) and a letter to Heads of other schools are the usual means of announcing the vacancy.

The 'job spec' can often be the weakest part of the process. Virtually all schools will aspire to the same mantra of waiting lists, academic success, pastoral care, sporting and cultural width and financial stability. But is there a development plan, which will tie the new Head's hands? Does the board have a strategic view of how the school should develop over the next decade? In some cases, there is a danger of seeking the opposite of the departing Head as a matter of course: this needs to be avoided.

The application forms must be approved by the school's lawyers, and then the submitted applications should be considered by the appointment committee. At this stage, there is benefit in having a scoring system, which results in the selection of four groups. The OPQR groupings

(Obvious, Possible, Questionable and Ridiculous) have an attraction. Ideally a list of eight to ten candidates will form this long list and these interviews will take place off campus. The same amount of time for each candidate – usually one hour – should allow an examination of the candidate's career, aspirations and ability to think logically in a crisis.

Round one and subsequently

This first round of interviews is seeking to establish a short list – ideally of three or four – whom the whole Board will interview later: it is not making an appointment. The adviser should guide the panel as to the questions that should be asked and, if required, produce a 'challenging scenario' to test the candidates' ability to analyse and act logically. Internal candidates must be treated in exactly the same way as all other candidates. Specific areas to explore at the second interview should be established and the adviser should take detailed notes, so that a frank but helpful debriefing of the unsuccessful candidates can be made. All applicants deserve this.

Too frequently, governors assume that all candidates will be honoured if they are offered the job, but it is vital to allow the candidates the time to ask questions and to visit the school – perhaps anonymously. It can also be beneficial for two governors to visit the applicants in their schools – but this is probably more useful if the applicant is already a Head.

Round two

The second round of interviews can take many different forms. While some Boards wish to interview again away from the school, most will wish to interview at the school and include in the process a social event with staff, and sometimes with some carefully chosen parents. As a candidate, it can seem as if you are a prize steer at Smithfield, and it also allows a common room sweepstake to flourish, but it does let the board see how the candidates fare in a public setting. Several schools now include an interview with a panel of pupils: this can be very revealing.

All the interviews should be well planned, with governors being given clear areas of questioning and the leading role being taken by those governors who were not involved in the first round of interviews. Again the adviser should play a role in deciding the thrust of the questioning.

Candidates must be given sufficient time to ask questions.

Some boards incline towards delegating the entire process to a sub-committee, but there are dangers in this. Whether or not all the governors are present at the final interviews, it is highly desirable that they have had the opportunity to meet the candidates, and perhaps to hear them give any formal presentations that have been asked for. It is essential that all governors feel that they have been fully involved somewhere in the process, and both can and will support an appointment being made. They must have no grounds for being able to become half-hearted about the appointment at a later stage, or even to go into denial that they approved it. Collective responsibility is the hallmark of any board.

If there is doubt or division, the board must be brave enough not to make an appointment. 'Going round again' is not a sign of weakness; indeed there is much truth in the old saying: 'Appoint in haste; repent at leisure.' But the headhunter or the advisers will need to change their strategy to get new applicants.

The outside assessor should provide a briefing note for all members of the Board about the references that have been gathered (both formally and informally). S/he should also have spoken to the candidates; guided them in the light of their performance in the first round of interviews; established if there are any major issues in their minds that need to be raised and addressed, and again kept detailed notes of the interview.

After the selection

Following these final interviews, some boards wish to make an announcement rapidly. This requires the financial package; the tenure; the CRB checks; the timing of future appraisals; and the announcement itself being agreed. Most schools require a medical examination but its nature and legal status is open to considerable debate. Membership of the various Heads' organisations (such as HMC, GSA, SHMIS, ISA, IAPS) is usually dependent on a contract being broadly in line with the AGBIS model contract, so work on this needs to be started well in advance of the final round of interviews. It is also useful to list all those individuals and groups who need to be informed, and to establish an effective process to ensure that this happens smoothly. It is an extremely sensitive issue.

After the public announcement, too many boards sit back and think that their role is over. But they need to support both the outgoing Head and also the newly appointed one. The school cannot be allowed to slip into a moratorium. So how can they ensure that the achievements of the outgoing Head are acknowledged and celebrated? How will the new Head be introduced and welcomed? Are there family or housing issues to resolve? Who is responsible for the creation of the next budget? What role will each of the Heads play in new staff appointments? One school set up a 'transition group' of two governors and three senior staff to help this process: an interesting idea.

The big question

In the 19th century, candidates used to present collections of testimonials when applying for headships, and sometimes had to deliver sermons to the board of governors. Now there are firms that help to improve candidates' CVs and applications, while some boards use psychometric tests and graphologists – so the process does evolve and change. But ultimately it remains a simple question of judgement: 'Have we found someone who is equipped to lead the school successfully in the years ahead?'

b) Professional headhunters

Chris Tongue

Over the past 20 years countless changes have taken place in schools, reflecting the increasing complexity of professional life. A typical Head is now supported by a senior management team; a typical governing body has a detailed sub-committee structure, and schools now employ experts in their fields to assist them with HR, public relations and marketing. The trend, therefore, to use headhunters – professional executive search and selection agencies, to give them their proper titles – to assist governors with their most important task of appointing their next Head is hardly surprising. Such organisations have been widely used in business and commerce for decades and in more recent times sporting bodies such as MCC and the RFU have sought help in this way.

The task

The task of recruiting a Head is a daunting one and, as is frequently pointed out, is the key one facing a governing body. In most schools, few governors possess significant experience of headship recruitment (why should they?) and, whilst governors may know their own school well, few will have a detailed knowledge of the independent sector as a whole (why should they?). Most Boards therefore welcome professional assistance: partly to guide them through the entire process from start to finish; partly to provide re-assurance that the appointment is being managed professionally and fairly; partly to relieve the school of an additional administrative burden; partly to re-assure their parents that they are taking the business of finding their next Head seriously; and partly in the hope that their professional headhunting assistant may be able to help attract a really strong field of candidates – some of whom might not otherwise submit an application.

I believe all parties are likely to benefit from a school using a good headhunter.

Parents

Most parents select their schools with discernment and will set aside the time to look at three or more schools for their children's education. Indeed, as a new Head, I once (foolishly) asked a prospective parent how many schools he was considering and received the answer 'four in Surrey, three in Kent, three in Sussex and one in Somerset'! I never asked that question again...

Parents will wish to meet – and find out all that they can about – the Head, and often it is the personality and standing of the Head that will determine the choice of school. When a Head's retirement is announced, a sense of insecurity will spread all too quickly amongst the community – for obvious reasons – and pupil recruitment can suffer until the new incumbent has established him/herself. By being seen to have a modern and professional approach to appointing the next Head, a board of governors can go a long way towards allaying such fears. Parents and others might also welcome the element of objectivity that the use of a headhunter is likely to bring to the process.

The staff

When a new Head is being appointed, it is also a nervous time for the staff, as they also need re-assurance that the governors are leaving no stones unturned to recruit the best possible Head. A headhunter can be invited to visit the school in advance of advertisements appearing in the press, to meet senior staff and to get their views on the needs of the school at that stage in its development. The headhunter can also provide re-assurance on the thoroughness of the process to be adopted. At a later stage, a few key senior staff may also be asked to meet short-listed candidates so that the latter are well informed prior to their final interviews. A shrewd Chairman can then get the impressions of senior staff ahead of the appointment to further the probability of an appointment being made that is a good fit for the school. The Chairman would be wise, however, not to ask staff for their order of preference!

Administrative back up

There is inevitably a lot of administration involved in a headship appointment. To have all this work done by a consultancy frees the school's administrators – including the hard-pressed bursar and/or clerk to the governors – to get on with their normal work. It also guarantees a degree of confidentiality for the candidates – an important consideration especially when current Heads are likely to be expressing an interest in a post.

Governors

Most boards do possess a range of professionals used to making appointments in their specialist fields. However, while there may be a Head or ex-Head on the board, there will be few with specific experience in headship selection. I have worked with a number of boards in recent years and few have really done their thinking, as regards the type of Head they are looking for, in advance of the start of the process. Do they, for example, seek to appoint someone who will build steadily and prudently upon the work of his/her predecessor and strive to enhance –

by incremental steps – the reputation of the school, or do they wish to appoint someone who will literally transform the school from the place it is now, to something that will be quite different in five years' time? Many boards simply want the 'best person for the job' but without having defined what the 'job' is that they wish to have done.

So what is the priority? Better pupil recruitment; improved academic performance; improved pastoral care; an enhanced co-curricular programme; fundamental curriculum change (to the IB or pre-U, say); or even a change of structure (single sex to coeducation or from boarding to day): all may feature at some stage in the governors' thinking. A headhunter can help to tease out priorities for the next phase of the school's development – if necessary.

A headhunter can also give practical advice on such things as the ideal timetable for the process – from advertisement to appointment – and the composition and size of the panel of governors to oversee the selection and interviewing right through to short-list stage (when normally all the board would be involved). The headhunter can also draft a selection of questions for the interviews; prepare a written exercise – if that is required – and suggest the format for a social function for making candidates and their spouses/partners feel welcome, enabling governors and candidates to get to know each other better in an informal setting. Most importantly, though, an experienced headhunter with a good network of contacts within the sector can help to attract a really strong field of candidates for the panel to consider for long-listing. And this is probably the key task in the whole process: without having a strong long-list of candidates, an outstanding appointment is unlikely to be made.

For potential candidates

A great many potential candidates will see the advertisements for a headship post, but relatively few will apply. Indeed, it is sometimes the case that the most prestigious schools attract the least number of candidates. Why is this? The best candidates for a leading school will be highly regarded Heads/senior staff who are greatly valued where they are, and who have spent time making a real mark and establishing their reputation in that school. Even assuming that the time is approaching when they should consider moving on, they will not wish to apply for another position unless they feel they have a good chance of being successful. Such candidates are far more likely to submit an application if approached by a headhunter and encouraged to apply, as this gives them the re-assurance that their application will be seriously considered; it also makes their conversations with their line manager (Chairman or Head) and other referees a great deal easier.

I have had countless such conversations with potential candidates, resulting in many cases in applications that have been successful. I have also managed to dissuade candidates from applying in cases where there was a clear mismatch – to the benefit of all parties. Finally, the headhunter is in the best position to give constructive feedback to unsuccessful candidates – at each stage – something that a caring school would certainly wish to be a key part of the overall process. Who knows: another more suitable post for that candidate might well arise before too long – and having an ongoing relationship with a key headhunter may be beneficial (for both parties).

The cost
Some governors and others will wonder if the cost of using a headhunter constitutes money well spent. This cost is usually calculated as a percentage of the first year's salary (the norm might be between 20-30% of that figure). This may seem a lot, but as a fraction of the year's turnover it is small, amounting to approximately the boarding fee for one pupil or the day fee for two – for just one year. On the other hand the cost of making a bad appointment may be astronomic – even amounting to a six- or even seven-figure sum. The use of a headhunter can therefore be seen as a type of insurance; a fee paid to minimise the chances – and consequences – of a disastrous appointment being made.

Possible disadvantages of using headhunters
It will be obvious from what I have already said that I believe headhunters can represent excellent value for money, in both the medium and long term, for a school. However, this does not mean that all schools should use them all of the time. Nor can I pretend that all headhunters have good knowledge of the independent sector or the right professional experience

or judgement. Nor do all headhunters always conform to good practice. I can think of a (very good) candidate being appointed to a (very good) school without any of his referees having been approached in advance of the formal offer being made: a most unusual happening that breaks all the safeguarding regulations. Governors will need to determine that a headhunter has all the essential qualities at the outset. A reputable headhunter will willingly put a Chairman in touch with other Chairmen for whom s/he has worked, and there is nothing more reassuring than a personal recommendation.

Finally, a board of governors might feel that by using a headhunter it risks losing control over the selection process. Once again, the key lies in using a good one: one who is thorough and professional and who will work closely with the Chairman throughout the process. It must always be the *governors* who decide who is to be long-listed: who is to go through to short-listing and who is to be appointed; the head-hunter's role is to provide support, guidance and experience and to ensure that the governors have a truly strong list of candidates from which to make their initial selection.

Summary

I believe that all schools should consider using headhunters with their headship appointments; that the Chairman (with one or two colleagues) should invite proposals from two or three agencies; speak to other Chairmen who have used their preferred agency and then decide whether or not to go down this route.

Yet, when all is said and done, one always returns to the central point with which this chapter began: whatever method of selection a school uses, the appointment of a new Head is far and away the most important role of any governing body.

Chapter 17

Governors and Heads: some potential disaster scenarios

Nigel Richardson

The Head, faced across the study desk by a 14-year-old who has been caught smoking, can be certain of one thing. Whatever the disciplinary sanctions being handed out and however courteously they are received, any well-meant advice about the causes of lung cancer will be met with a faint but perceptible glazing over of the teenage eyes. Why? Because in the pupil's view one thing is certain: premature death only ever happens to *other* people.

It is exactly the same with schools and governors. We may hear local rumours or read in the press about parent dissatisfaction and discord here; a governor-Head falling out there; a sudden departure and scandal somewhere else – but such things only happen in schools less successful and well-ordered than the one *we* help to govern.

Maybe it's just as well that most teenagers feel this way: the young ought to have time to dream their dreams, and the belief in being immortal is part of that optimism. Governors, too, ought to embark on their new role confident that all will go well and that anything is possible. Yet this confidence needs also to have just a tinge of awareness that harmony won't *automatically* be permanent. Our forebears sometimes lamented in retrospect over the way in which England seemed to have slipped into civil war almost un-noticed in the early 1640s; a significant number of governing bodies have gone through a parallel experience.

So, never assume that what paragraphs 3.28-3.34 of the 2011 edition of AGBIS's publication *Guidelines for Governors* describe (under the rather coy overall heading of 'Troubled Relationships') are something that will only happen to other people. Be realistic, too, about the fact that, life being essentially unfair, schools with high-quality governors and Heads won't necessarily be the ones that cruise effortlessly on their way without mishap.

However, lest what follows seems rather bleak, this chapter comes with one very strong initial assertion: it deals with worst case scenarios, and as a proportion of Heads appointed, those who take what is known in sporting parlance as the 'early bath' are very much in the minority. Just how much of a minority is, of course, hard to say: percentage statistics about how many Heads leave their school prematurely, either voluntarily or under duress, are difficult to determine, because the process often takes place surrounded by confidentiality, out of respect and sensitivity for all concerned.

Prevention is better than cure

How does one minimise the risk? Many of the means of prevention have been described in earlier chapters: careful recruitment of a new Head, using external advice if necessary; sound committee structures, terms of reference and processes; effective reporting and communication; good succession planning and the skilful choice of governors, based on a varied skills-set and identified by an effective nominations committee.

Some external mechanisms already exist, too, for ensuring that a school does not slip in standards or effectiveness without governors being aware that it is happening. When regular inspection of independent schools began in the 1990s, it was not unknown for the inspectors to depart on a Friday after the feedback session to governors, and for the Head to follow them out of the door on a Monday. Several cycles further on, it is now much less likely that a governing body will suddenly discover that its school has been failing over a long period under a seriously ineffective Head. A variety of sources of consultancy are available where particular areas of a school seem to give cause for concern (AGBIS and HMC can advise governors and Heads respectively on this matter).

The appraisal systems for both Heads and governing bodies described in the next two chapters are designed to give governors some additional valuable sources of information about the quality of leadership in their school. Much more written guidance is available about governance than in times past, and there are many more AGBIS seminars for governors at all levels, ranging from experienced Chairmen to first-time board members.

While, for the best of reasons, governing bodies often want newly-arriving Heads to be able to assess their surroundings and situation for themselves rather than being saddled with preconceptions from the Board too early, it is possible to lean too far the other way. New Heads need at least some broad parameters. Even though such guidelines are a matter primarily for Chairmen to impart, they will need to take their Board with them, and to ensure that all governors are 'on message' about them.

Has the successful candidate been appointed to preside over change or continuity? If it is to be the former, is it by evolution or revolution? Has the Board already set any key priorities for the future? Are there key issues on which the governing body expects to be consulted before any change takes place, or even before any parent or staff consultation is launched? School uniform is one example: Heads' training courses wisely counsel participants to be cautious about assuming that their board will take a compliant attitude on this issue.

Never over-estimate a new Head's experience of dealing with a board and its business. At one time no 'ordinary' teacher, even a deputy, went near the board at all; nowadays many deputies will have attended a board committee in their former school and some will have been to the board itself. However, some will never have done either – and even if they have, being in the hotseat now is very different from their previous experience of being (probably) essentially an observer. They may well need guidance on board procedure and expectation.

How does the board define the line between day-to-day management (which is the Head's responsibility) and longer-term strategy (for which governors are responsible)? Does it require termly or annual reports on exam results, discipline and staff changes? In what form, and on which topics, does the board expect papers to be presented to it by the new Head?

The newcomer will probably have access to reports drawn up by the previous Head; but should the departed Head's style and *modus operandi* automatically be continued or could things be done better? Does the board want to know more about (say) projected pupil numbers for the next two years and just a little less about the results of the 4th junior colts? Might the start of the new era be a good time to drop the 'My Lords and Gentlemen' style of address with which the Head's written report still begins in a few schools, in favour of a slightly more modern approach? It will be a brave newcomer who takes it upon him/herself to take such an initiative, but with a little encouragement from above...

It is also worth considering whether the board should contain at least one experienced or recently retired Head, and whether, in addition to the Head and bursar/clerk, other SMT members should attend at least some of the committees – for example, the deputies, the junior school head and the marketing or development director. After all, the executives – usually just two: Head and bursar – appearing before the board on their own are far more heavily outnumbered by non-executives (governors) than would be the case in many commercial organisations. On the other hand, one can justify this practice by the fact that the board's relationship with this pair is a very particular one, given the terms of their employment: in practice they are answerable to the board in a way in that assistant staff are not.

Resist the temptation to exclude the Head and bursar from sessions of 'private business' unless there is a *very* good reason to do so (some salary issues; appointment of successors *etc*). Such sessions can be very unsettling for those who are asked to leave, and they can give rise to rumour and misunderstanding unless the Chairman afterwards explains the reasons for such a session to those who have been asked to withdraw. The executive's members need to be fully in touch with governors' thinking: they need to be on hand to explain the impractical or impossible and it will be left to them to enact the decisions (or to pick up the pieces) after the governors have left. Remember Sir Humphrey in *Yes, Minister,* having discovered Jim Hacker's latest bright idea only from others, rather than from the minister himself: "I always said we should never let them [*ie* the politicians] out at weekends..."

Testing times: the most likely scenarios

No two schools are quite the same, and the circumstances in which trouble can overtake them will be similarly varied. Nevertheless, based on case studies over the years, it is possible to identify six broad categories. Some are much more straightforward than others, and they can appear in isolation or in combination with each other.

1) The Head (new or experienced) has done or said something beyond the pale. This may fall under the legal definition of gross misconduct, and it might well consist of inappropriate behaviour towards children – but it could also include (for example) fraudulent or other criminal action, and offensive or hare-brained actions or comments after having too much to drink. Whatever the origin, it has probably caused a situation in which the Head's position is untenable and irretrievable, and in which the school cannot flourish until s/he is replaced.

As difficult situations go, this category is comparatively straightforward – assuming that everyone on the board agrees where the 'pale' begins and ends. There is much to be said for the board, firmly led by its Chairman, acting quickly and decisively. However, good legal advice should be taken to minimise the risk of the school having to appear before an employment tribunal for wrongful dismissal or incurring some other form of legal action for allegedly causing the loss of the Head's livelihood. If there is any risk of short-term adverse PR or long-term reputational risk to the school, getting specialist PR support may be advisable (see chapter 2 of volume 6 in this series): this will not come cheap, but it may be well worth it in the long run.

Parents and other supporters of the school appreciate honesty in such circumstances, but they also tend to respect the reasons why a board cannot be completely open: what they tend to dislike is any suspicion of secrecy for secrecy's sake. It is also worth bearing in mind that the extent to which they will trust governors in a crisis depends on how confident they were feeling about the governing body's competence and communication skills *before* this situation broke: effective communication in the good times pays dividends in the bad ones.

2) The new face does not fit after all, and never will. However carefully a board goes about appointing a new Head, a successful fit cannot be totally guaranteed, and it is always possible that the new arrival (especially in a first headship) will turn out to be far less well-equipped than the supporting referees said or thought, or than the candidate seemed at interview.

Big surprises along these lines are mercifully unusual – but this depends on the original selection process having been properly handled. Where they do occur, and if the board is sure that the situation is irrevocable, it may be best for all concerned if it is quickly resolved rather than being allowed to limp on, however painful that may be in the short-term. Nevertheless there can be no getting away from the fact that when it does happen, there has been a failure of governance, from which the board must seek to draw the right lessons for the future: it is only fair on the clutch of candidates next time around that the procedures are improved, and (to misquote Oscar Wilde's Lady Bracknell's views on parents) for a board to lose one appointee might look like a misfortune, whereas to lose two in quick succession will seem, in PR terms, like something a lot worse than carelessness.

In some cases the failure of face-fit may be for reasons that lie largely outside the Head's control. The board's collective *persona* may turn out to be incompatible with his/hers; indeed, from a Head's point of view the individual and collective chemistry of his or her new employers can seem a terrifyingly random phenomenon. Occasionally the new Head arrives to find that the Chairman and many of the board members have changed since the appointment was made.

In such situations especially, one of the prime aims should be to safeguard the Head's future career, even if s/he is going to have to leave this job – of which, more towards the end of this chapter. This includes a financial pay-off/safety net while the Head finds a new post, and going the extra mile to support – frankly and truthfully –- any future application that the Head may make elsewhere.

However, it is also worth entering lots of other *caveats* before any governing body rushes into precipitate action. First, there is much truth in the idea (once stated to me by the Chairman of a school in the USA) that "Boards appointing Heads are always looking for God on a good day". Even the best and most experienced Heads are rarely brilliant at *every* aspect of their very multi-faceted role.

Secondly, new Heads need to be given time. They cannot solve everything – nor address every individual governor's personal agenda – in the first term or even the first year. They embark on a huge learning curve. They may well meet 5000 or more new people in their first year, whether they are new to headship or seasoned campaigners changing schools.

Even the best-prepared, dynamic young deputy taking on his/her first headship has to come to terms with the reality of the loneliness of the person at the top; the competing demands on time; all the new ways and expectations about how things are done in new surroundings; the loss for both Head and spouse of old friends in one's former school; the need to get one's family rooted in a new house, and one's own children settled into new schools. Many new Heads are surprised by the extent to which their 'street-cred' does *not* follow them from their last school and has to be re-earned.

They may well have had much less experience of handling a board than you assume. So beware of overwhelming them, of becoming the constant questioner, and the one who rings up every time you see a hanging-out shirt within five miles of the school. Beware too of adopting the tempting but dangerous role of governor-rhetorician: the governor who can swing a meeting with a few clever sound bites.

Moreover the experienced Head that has been hugely successful in a first headship may well face different but equally demanding new challenges in a second one. It is quite likely that in the former post there will have been a relatively strong sense of hierarchy, with both staff and governors content for the Head to make many of the strategic and other decisions more or less alone and unchallenged. The dynamics – and politics – may be quite different when s/he arrives in, for example, a household-name day-school with a common room that contains a number of talented but individualist senior staff who have made a conscious choice *not* to seek headships themselves, or in a much larger boarding school with houses (and powerful housemasters/mistresses) dispersed around a town, and an ethos that is much more collegiate (if you approve of it) or baronial (if you don't).

3) The Head is evidently no longer able to do the job, through illness, stress etc. The key word here is 'evidently'. Wherever possible, it is best to proceed by agreement: competence procedures for Heads inevitably involve subjective judgements and can be messy and far from clear-cut.

Agreement tends to be much simpler if governors and Head have already worked together to ensure ongoing and regular appraisal, and that the Head already has a good career/retirement plan and pension arrangements. Governors should ensure that the Head has consulted his/her professional association and that s/he has had access to the best possible pensions advice. Enhancement for ill-health can be given under the teachers' pension scheme, subject to proper medical evidence.

Above all, remember that in this situation the Head's immediate family may well have emotional and material needs, too – and they too may well experience a deep sense of loss as they have to leave the school community (especially their home is a tied house at the centre of it) – and an uncertain future if the Head is seriously ill.

4) Maybe it's time for a change. This category is more elusive than the previous one, and notoriously more pitfall-prone. Sometimes it takes place against a background of slipping numbers, with some governors, especially those from business organisations in which performance can be more readily assessed statistically, feeling that marketing is insufficiently imaginative or aggressive or that 'nettles are just not being grasped' on matters of individual staff performance. Too often it starts with a dip in league table placings – never a very reliable measure of a school's performance or that of its Head, if taken in isolation from other indicators. Whatever the reason, where it happens it tends to be given a label that became familiar in the recession of the early 1990s: 'the football manager syndrome'.

This is the scenario in which to draw to the full on the evidence that can be drawn from inspection and appraisal. Look before you leap, and be mindful of the reputational risks of upheaval; bear in mind the possibility of constructive dismissal allegations if you voice your doubts and simply de-stabilise the Head in the eyes of parents. In such situations, everyone on the board should also ask themselves and each other some simple questions. Have we got an accurate perception of the downsides compared with the upsides? Are we sure that the downsides are actually the fault of the Head? Does the board have a role alongside the Head in retrieving the situation? Are we *sure* that the answer lies in a change of face at the top?

As with most of the other scenarios, if the parting of the ways can be achieved sensitively, quietly and by agreement, there may well be benefits both for the Head and the school. In some cases the governing body may be able to signal discreetly that the Head should look to find other work within a certain period of time – *but* there are risks of alleged constructive dismissal, and this approach should never be undertaken without very careful legal advice.

Before moving on, it is worth pointing out that scenarios 3 and 4 seem increasingly likely to occur as pension arrangements change and an increasing number of Heads and others work well into their 60s. Some of them will by then have been in the job for well over two decades. The independent sector has never been able to offer Heads the secondment opportunities that many high-flying maintained sector counterparts have enjoyed, and sabbatical leave is becoming rarer. In tough economic times, schools (especially boarding schools) are more likely to say that they cannot spare the Head from recruiting even for a few weeks – yet the need for some Heads to be able to recharge the batteries will never have been greater. It is an issue that needs serious thought and discussion from governors and Heads right across the sector in the years ahead.

5) Controversy over the speed and management of change. In many ways this is the most complex scenario of all – and one which, over time, has occurred all too often. Frequently it is prompted by pressure groups of staff and/or parents lobbying governors, and governors listening too readily. Things may be exacerbated by a governor who is on the board because s/

he has been nominated by the staff, but who listens to their concerns too uncritically and behaves more as a delegate than a representative.

Managing change is much written about, but sometimes highly difficult to achieve without pain and resistance. Too often it follows a long regime, in which the governors (who have often known no other Head) have decided, out of respect for the legend about to retire, to 'leave all the changes for the next one'. All too frequently when the change does eventually start to come, it turns out to be a two-stage process, with the short-lived, transitional initiator swept away in the controversy (Mikhail Gorbachev), and second newcomer eventually 'doing the business' (Boris Yeltsin).

One of the things that most struck me whilst doing research into the governance of American schools a decade ago was their willingness to employ very experienced Heads as short-term or 'interim' post-holders for three years or so to draw the sting of change: British independent schools have tended too often to throw the inexperienced newcomer in at the deep end and then to appoint an interim Head only after the crisis has followed.

Moreover, in guarding the institutions they love, the British are more prone to nostalgia than most: remember the old joke question about the Church of England: 'How many Anglicans does it take to change a light-bulb?' The answer: '100 – one to change the bulb and 99 to say how much more they liked the old one.' In such situations in schools too, self-appointed 'keepers of the ethos' tend to emerge: sometimes they are long-standing members of staff or well-meaning former pupils; sometimes parents who take only a short-term (*ie* until our child leaves) view of what is right for the school, rather than the governors' longer-term, strategic vision. Final-year pupils can be prone to this as well: after all, they will continue to see the departed legend as 'our Head', and to wish that s/he had stayed on to see out their own time in the school.

This is the scenario par excellence that demands sound judgement; calm and measured actions and a sense of proportion from every governor. Is the pressure group actually representative? Is it an example of how people sometimes exercise power without responsibility? Or is this group voicing concerns that we have not thought of; have underestimated, and ignore at our peril? Have we been sure to tell parents to refer their concerns to the Head in the first instance, rather than allowing ourselves to be a back-door route for complaints? Any governor who has particular responsibility for staff matters can be especially in the firing line in such situations.

This is also where governors can exercise one of their most important functions: as a shelter behind which the Head can stand as they take the rap for whatever controversial change is being enacted.

This set of circumstances may also be accompanied by...

6) A governing body increasingly divided into groups or factions. Again, the divisions may take several forms. Some boards become split along generational lines – especially where former pupils constitute a high proportion of the governors. Some allow 'a board within a board' to grow up, turning the other members into ciphers – for example, if a single F&GP or executive committee takes all the key decisions. In an age when the cost of large building projects has to be carefully monitored, a governors' project steering group can run similar risks: it tends to contain the biggest movers and shakers from the board, and the Head feels increasingly that s/he is in fact working to two different governing bodies that do not always fully cohere.

Once again the role of a strong and effective Chairman is crucial in avoiding such trends, so it is perhaps unsurprising that there seems to be an increased risk of factionalism where the Chairman appoints a new Head and then steps down too soon after s/he arrives, or where the Chairman and the chairman of F&GP do not get on. One well-known school that got into difficulties did so partly because the board Chairman did not attend the F&GP committee, and the committee chairman became *de facto* an alternative authority. The Head never knew where he stood, and the board eventually split down the middle.

General principles
Whichever scenario, singly or in combination, life throws at you, there are some common principles that will benefit all concerned.

- Whatever the circumstances, the school's governance articles must be followed, and Head's contractual rights must be respected – including the right to a fair appeal hearing.

- Where necessary, there should be compromise and confidentiality agreements to safeguard the interests of both sides. However, if the case involves child protection the governors cannot evade their responsibility to inform the appropriate safeguarding agency.

- It is important for the Chairman to communicate fully with other board members, and to take them with him/her. In return, board members have a very important contribution to make in terms of their corporate loyalty once decisions have been made, and in their ability to keep things confidential and to maintain a united public front.

- Where there is a parting of the ways, it will nearly always have been a deeply wounding experience to the individual and family at the centre of it. In cases where a controversial appointment has resulted in a polarisation – whether it be between supporters and opponents within the board, the common room or the parent body, there will be plenty of institutional scars too. These will take time and effort to heal, along with the damage to the school's reputation.

- There are sometimes no winners and many losers: even those who were happy to foment some of the trouble in the first place, or to help it on its way, often end up being caught up in its wake. A wise governing body usually tries to ensure that anyone who has led a common room coup does not end up unduly benefiting from it once the dust has settled.

When appointing your *next* Head, don't automatically rule out someone who has been through a short-lived headship, but do some very careful homework amongst referees and grapevines. An increasing number of Heads have been through a torrid early experience, only to make a rather better fist of a later one, and the membership of the 'second chance club' of Heads includes a larger number of the Great and Good than people often realise.

Maybe some of those club members were fortunate that the boards with whom they once fell out were discreet and leak-proof at the time. A number of us have, over the years, lived to fight another day (Dear

Reader: I was one such...), thanks to understanding and supportive referees who recommended us for a new headship within a short space of time – and to governing bodies that were prepared to be open-minded about our past. But if you do place your faith in someone who has been through such an experience, be prepared to put a careful PR strategy in place around the announcement of your appointment, to pre-empt any negative parental reaction.

And finally

There should always be some creative tension between governors and Head (or bursar, for that matter). I emphasise 'creative' but some tension there should always be, for the effective board will always be the one that provides at least a little grit in the oyster.

It is sometimes said that one of the greatest risks to a school comes in the final years of a hugely successful, long-serving Head: the governing body becomes *too* harmonious – as it becomes packed with the Legend's friends and think-a-likes. But then again, compared with some of the scenarios already described, this can be a nice problem to have.

The old saying: 'Mr X departed as he had arrived: fired with enthusiasm' has a certain ring to it, but it cannot hide the fact that a great deal of unproductive time and energy, money and pain will have gone into the process. Avoid it if you possibly can, and remember: prevention is indeed better than cure.

Chapter 18

Appraisal of Heads and senior staff

Chris Brown

I was a Head for a considerable number of years. For all but one of those years, I had the same Chairman: a delightful, intelligent, cultured man. In his younger years, on National Service, he had won an MC. He came from a privileged family, and believed that with privilege comes the responsibility to serve society. Apart from being a governor of my school, he had been a JP, a county councillor, for a while chairman of the local police authority, chairman of a national park, regional chairman and then a national figure in the National Trust. The list could go on. Interestingly, in his later years he became ordained.

As 'my' Chairman, he was all one might ask: he conveyed a sense of trust, and left the bursar and myself to manage the running of the school; he saw which were important issues; he was concerned about effective financial controls, but also realised that schools are about more than the bottom line. If problems arose, he was invariably supportive. I did, and do, regard him highly and with affection.

Each year before the start of the new academic year, we would meet for a brief review of my role as Head. Looking back on those conversations, I remember that they were supportive and relatively brief, but if I am honest with myself, whilst they may have been reassuring, they did not help me grow as a professional.

The tables now are turned. In my semi-retirement, I have undertaken a considerable number of appraisals for Heads. Indeed, I now meet each year with others involved in such work to discuss how the process can be improved. It has become ever clearer to me how much better the support and guidance is for Heads than when I began. Many more training opportunities exist: the Heads' associations undertake preliminary training courses; offer mentors who are existing Heads; indeed much more emphasis is given to leadership in schools in all sectors. Thus, it is now much more common practice, even if not yet obligatory, for appraisal of Heads to be undertaken.

Appraisal as the norm

This is in a context where in organisations across the country and in schools in particular, appraisal is now the norm for employees and staff. Inspection of schools asks questions about the appraisal system, and indeed how well it is linked with professional development and training. For a Head not to be appraised when all the teaching staff is would seem illogical, and is hardly setting the right example.

Historically the system I experienced obtained in many schools. It is a truth now more universally acknowledged that the Chairman is not necessarily best placed to undertake the role. S/he will know the Head well and will certainly have a view on how the individual is performing, but won't usually have been a Head. Even if s/he has been, s/he might feel reticent about asserting that his/her own past style was the only way of doing things. Furthermore, having someone from outside the school brings a degree of objectivity, and experience of having undertaken the role that most Chairmen cannot bring. Inspection now expects to give objective comment on the leadership and management of the school. For the Chairman to have a document that is the basis for a discussion allows issues to be raised impersonally that might otherwise be sensitive to bring up.

The best way forward

So what is the system I am advocating? First of all, it is important for any appraiser to indicate to Head and Chairman that the exact style of the process can be determined by them. Such wishes may be put in the context of what such appraisal usually entails. It should also be said that variations on the theme are, of course, possible. An appraiser can involve a governor in the process agreed. I know of one school where the senior management as a whole was examined by an expert from the commercial world rather than the academic one. So while I am outlining a particular approach, others are clearly possible.

It should be said that it is helpful to agree terms at the outset so that no surprises arise. I usually indicate the region of the likely sum but say that I calculate the fee in relation to a daily rate and the eventual sum may alter for that reason. Given that at least three to four days are involved in the visit to the school, the preparatory and subsequent report writing will add up to at least a week's work. The only other expenses are travel to the school and accommodation whilst there. I have not felt it appropriate to stay with the Head. It is sensible for governors to allow for such a sum in the budget.

I normally expect to meet the Chairman in advance of my visiting the school. It is helpful to develop a relationship; it is also important to ensure that any points the Chairman or the governors wish to have explored are known to me.

Gathering the evidence

The process normally includes a self-appraisal by the Head, responding to a series of questions. These include what s/he sees as his or her priorities; the nature of relationships with key groups; communication; the particular achievements and failures experienced, and what has been learned. The patterns of work; the management of time; involvement in different aspects of the school; strengths and weaknesses are all explored. The questions allow for any particular concern or issue to be raised by the Head.

Questionnaires are sent to governors, often followed up later with phone calls to a certain number. A similar but different questionnaire is sent to a cross-section of parents, with the aim of about 50 being approached, but chosen entirely randomly – that is, say, every tenth name on the list. Responses from both these groups are sent direct to the appraiser. Next, questionnaires are sent to all teaching staff and a cross-section of non-teaching. I think in many schools that celebrate their sense of community, the latter is important.

If a school has a number of significant feeder schools, half a dozen may be approached via questionnaire, though I prefer to make contact by phone. If the school admits most of its pupils from the maintained sector at 11-plus and pupils are drawn from a large number of feeders, it is less appropriate or manageable to do. Some advocate contact with former pupils, but I am less convinced, since such individuals tend to view the school as it was, not as it is or is aspiring to be. I have, however, spoken with the officers of such an association if the link is close and a working relationship exists.

The appraiser is also sent all the relevant documentation: the prospectus; the most recent ISI report (and report on boarding if applicable); the development plan, and, with the agreement of Chairman and Head, the three most recent reports to governors. Finally anything the Head thinks important is included. The school website is also a helpful source.

The appraisal visit
So before visiting the school, I as an appraiser have a very considerable amount of information and a lot of views of the Head from different groups. In arranging a visit to the school, I usually expect to arrive by, say, Monday lunchtime and leave on Thursday morning, having given the Head an oral feedback about what would be in the report. I ask that my timetable would include seeing the Head in any routine activity: taking assembly; chairing an SMT meeting, or speaking to a group of parents. Such events are placed in my timetable first.

I ask to be shown round the school by some senior pupils, to get a feel for the school and a sense of how they feel about their life at the school. I don't ask directly about their views of the Head, but often such things emerge. In one recent instance the Head specifically asked that I should meet a group over lunch and talk with them about him and his role. Inevitably it is only a small group and may not be representative.

The bulk of the time at the school is spent in interviews with members of staff, principally teaching staff. I ask that the Head submits those whom I should meet; the senior team, including the bursar, head of junior or prep school and so forth. I then ask that the member of the senior team responsible for appraisal should select a cross-section of others representing differing ages, posts of responsibility, but always including some who are young and new to the school, and include at least one common room grumbler. It should be seen that those interviewed are not chosen by the Head alone.

By these means, you have put together a 360 degree perspective on the Head and the work he does. I should add, I usually ask to meet the Head's husband or wife; in exploring the Head's working practices, it is often helpful to ensure that the whole truth of what Heads ask of themselves is explored! I also wish to talk to the Head's PA, principally about how they work together; how the mountain of emails is managed; how effective the processes are.

In meeting members of staff, it is important to reassure them that their comments and responses will be treated confidentially. Some are often nervous that what they say may return to their employer and people can be understandably anxious. It is important to create an atmosphere of trust. Even the critical see the demands and difficulties of a Head's role. In my experience if you show you want to listen, people are candid and open. It is a privilege to go into a school and explore matters with such freedom.

It is, however, worth emphasising that an appraiser's judgements must sometimes be quite subtle. Does the negative parent have a genuine concern, or merely a particular axe to grind? Should the appraiser listen to the Head or to the staffroom critic? Often, of course, it is the nuances, the shades of grey, that lead to a helpful perception, rather than one extreme or the other.

Debriefing the Head

The final interview with the Head is clearly important. The most assured individual may well have some anxiety after the appraiser has had such free rein in learning so much and being privy to many confidences. It is also my experience that most Heads are very self-critical, and listen more readily to any suggestions for adjustment before absorbing all the information that is positive. If issues have arisen about the school that have come to my notice and where I can offer advice or suggestion, or point to good practice elsewhere, I do so without their forming part of the report. It is also the time to discuss any issues arising from the self-evaluation.

The main focus, however, is on the appraisal and its contents. It is often an opportunity for the Head to discuss matters that he or she feels cannot be aired with the governors, or how to deal with some particularly intractable problem. It is also important to ensure there is time for the Head to respond to, put in context or discuss any issue that has arisen in the draft report. And indeed discussion about next career steps or the moment for retirement can be aired. Such meetings rarely take less than two hours.

When suggesting areas for improvement or professional development, the appraiser needs to make a careful judgement between advice that is obviously useful, both for the Head in his present circumstances and for his future development, and that which is impractical or unlikely to be achievable. Suggesting that a Head with Luddite tendencies should acquire greater IT skills; suggesting to someone whose conscientiousness far outweighs his charisma that his public speaking skills can be transformed overnight by a short course may be somewhat less helpful. On the other hand finding strategies for improvement in either case may be worthwhile.

Reflections from experience
Having undertaken a number of such appraisals, it is interesting that certain issues recur: the management of working time; making time for strategic thinking; getting around the school; making best use of the Head's PA; creating trust and ensuring proper delegation; and not least, making time for private life.

I can't do better than quote Keith Dawson, himself a very experienced former Head in both the maintained and independent sectors, who from his experience of appraising many Heads wrote:

> The most precious aspect of an external appraisal is that it gives undivided time to listen to the Head outside the daily working relationships; to discuss his or her work, successes, problems and needs in what is a uniquely isolated and often lonely job.

The written report
I structure the report in a way that enables the thoughts of the various constituencies to be reflected. I use quotation but do not attribute it, and I cannot use comment that is attributable by deduction. Often helpful

or important points can be raised that are not necessarily part of my focus. I look to draw the whole together with my own observations, and highlighting issues that deserve some reflection or are areas that might help the Head to improve; to use time better; to improve the management of the school, or how s/he presents ideas. It is also important to look at the needs of the Head: some space for a personal life; time with spouse and family; sufficient respite to recharge batteries. By exploring these, and supporting the Head in seeking them, they are brought to the attention of the Chairman as well.

I look to establish at the outset of the whole process that the report is for the Head and Chairman only. I advise against suggesting that it might have a wider readership. I undertook an appraisal in one school where a major problem was the relationship between Head and bursar (not unique as a situation). If the report were to be seen by all governors, then the bursar as clerk to the governors (which is often the case) would read it, and a principal issue could not therefore be explored. It is entirely appropriate, however, for the Chairman to give an oral report to the next governors' meeting. If Head and Chairman subsequently agree for wider distribution, that is their decision. I also take the view that whilst I may make suggestions, specific target setting is the role of the Chairman. S/he is best placed to link these with the development plan. Some Chairmen ask appraisers to write a short summary report for board members.

The benefits

It seems to me that there are four principal benefits of the process I describe. The Head undertakes a self-evaluation that enables him or her to think about all aspects of what is done, and to reflect on failures as well as achievements. The members of staff at the school see that the Head is appraised, as they themselves are required to be; many comment that it is in a far more thorough manner. A great deal of affirmation and appreciation arises. Most people think it inappropriate to say 'well done' to the Head, so it is an important opportunity to point out so much that is good. Finally, suggestions about aspects that might be better or differently done can be explored. The oral feedback gives the Head an opportunity to correct or put in context issues that have arisen. I send the emended report to the Head first to allow time for further comment before sending it to the Chairman. The document can then form the basis for a discussion between Head and Chairman.

I indicated earlier that much more structure now exists to help a Head in the role. I see the nature of the process I have outlined as part of the Head's professional development. It is not an inspection report, but aims to affirm, whilst also pointing to means of further development. This is an important distinction. That said, one Head I appraised resigned shortly thereafter, so the process is not without rigour.

If the governors have real concerns about a Head, it is they who need to address the issue or issues. An appraisal report may point to matters; it is not the appraiser's role to resolve them. As I indicate later, appraisal and performance management are not the same things. Systems that seek to embrace both can have an unhelpful tension. Listening to the needs of the individual does not always sit easily with registering the requirements of the institution.

A distinguished mentor of mine in appraisal asked those he interviewed at a school a final question: "What one piece of advice would you give the Head?" A list of such comments given to the Head can form a helpful commentary of salient points and regularly include words of encouragement.

How often should a Head be appraised? It seems sensible that those setting out on headship need a certain time to establish themselves. Sometime in the third year of headship is about the right moment. Thereafter much depends on the individual case, the expected period of office and individual circumstances, but every three or four years is appropriate. The Heads' associations hold lists of people like myself who have some experience in this work.

Appraisal of the senior management team

Two other areas arise that can benefit from an external appraiser. The first relates to senior management teams. It can often be very helpful for an outsider to look at the structure and processes of such a team. It is worth reflecting that, some years ago, schools were run by the Head along with a senior deputy who had often been internally appointed. The increase in demands; legislation; the needs of compliance; the requirement to manage a more complex organisation; have all led to the need for larger co-operative teams.

Such teams, however, have quite often grown a little like Topsy, piecemeal, in response to need and as a result of individuals and their strengths. If that happens the demarcation of responsibility may not be as clear as should be, and is thus confusing to the staff when they look to seek help about a problem or issue. Clarity of structure does not exist. Job descriptions may not be similar in format or may not have been updated in response to the regular changes that in practice inevitably take place.

Perhaps most importantly, the principal areas of the school and its management are not systematically covered. Is the team in question advisory or executive? Also to be explored are the processes of the team. Are meetings effective, and sufficiently regular without being overbearing; are minutes taken; action points followed through? In short, does the system work effectively in managing the school? Is the group in fact senior, managing and a team? All these issues can be explored, based on reading the relevant paperwork, talking to those involved and seeing meetings in operation. It can be very helpful to Head and governors to have such a commentary, not always so clearly seen from the inside.

This leads me on to the appraisal of senior staff. Heads regularly undertake the appraisal of members of their senior team. The frequency of that depends on the system devised by the school. It is, however, a *regular* demand, and the use of an external appraiser can offer the Head some respite; bring in an outside voice, and demonstrate to the individual involved the care the school takes over such important matters.

How the process is undertaken can obviously vary. The approach developed by some colleagues and myself has several elements. The person in question undertakes a self-appraisal by responding to a series of questions posed. This always includes the opportunity to raise whatever concerns might be relevant. He or she then devises a short questionnaire to be sent to, say, five to ten relevant colleagues. The questionnaire can helpfully include the questions: 'What does X do well?' and 'What might X do better or differently?'

These completed questionnaires are sent direct to the appraiser. The job description is also sent. A visit to the school, lasting a day, includes interviews with some colleagues; perhaps an activity undertaken by the individual; but two meetings with the appraisee: one to explore the self-appraisal and the issues it may raise; the other being the final meeting covering this, the comments and suggestions of colleagues, and the observations of the appraiser. As with a Head, affirmation as well as suggestion is a part of the process; similarly it should be seen as part of continuing professional development. Advice about career development and training can also be included, though it is important to check first with the Head that this is acceptable territory. A report is then sent to the individual, and once agreed, sent to the Head.

These various forms of appraisal can serve to support governors in their work of developing their school, and also Heads and their senior managers, expecting them to be both self-critical and to bear in mind the needs of their professional development.

Chapter 19

Board appraisal and development: how AGBIS can help

Stuart Westley

For any readers unduly daunted by what has been described in previous chapters, fear not: help is at hand, in the form of the various services that AGBIS can offer to its member schools.

Essentially, these fall into the following categories:

• e-Learning

This is for both new and experienced governors, and is going through a process of continuous development – see chapter 1. Access to the course is straightforward. You will need to obtain a registration form either from the website or by calling the AGBIS office. On completion of the form a unique password will be issued that will remain active for six months. The training is available free of charge to governors of schools in membership.

• Seminars

Each year AGBIS organises a series of day-seminars in London and other regional centres. Details are sent regularly to all member schools via the clerk, and directly to those governors whose individual email addresses we hold. They can also be found on the AGBIS website under 'Seminars and Events'. Each year one of the five seminars held in London is designed for board Chairmen and one for newly appointed governors.

• Publications

Guidelines for Governors, referred to several times already in this book, has recently been revised. Copies may be downloaded from the website by governors of member schools; hard copies are available for purchase from the AGBIS office: £7 per copy for members.

• Other events

A variety of organisations provide training in various aspects of governance and they not infrequently request that AGBIS publicise their initiatives. This we are content to do, having no ambition to monopolise training but rather to engage with any initiative designed to assist governors. *We do not endorse other commercial products or enterprises and are committed to sending to governors only such information as relates directly to their responsibility as governors.*

• Advice to boards or individual governors

The AGBIS office maintains a telephone and email advice service for any schools that experience or anticipate difficulties.

Typical examples of our involvement are in recommending good practice; giving advice on a particular situation involving the conduct of an individual; on governing structures or board procedures. Sometimes we may need to advise you to seek specialist professional help. We need to remember that we are not lawyers

One example of an area of governance on which we increasingly give advice is over potential conflicts of interest: how to declare interests; how to avoid conflicts; how to deal with them when they do arise. Such conflicts can take many forms and they probably arise more frequently than is commonly supposed. Examples include governors who are also parents and who find themselves in dispute with their school; those who may have business links with their school; those who may wish to govern two schools or organisations whose interests may overlap or conflict.

• Reviews of governance

Self-review is an increasing feature and expectation in many professional walks of life, and is recommended as good practice to schools by the Charity Commission. Independent schools in some other parts of the world (*eg* the USA) have tended to be somewhat ahead of their British counterparts in this respect. **AGBIS strongly** recommends that governing bodies conduct a self-review exercise regularly and makes available to members via the website a simple document to assist in the process.

The main purposes of the exercise are to ensure:
- that governors' individual skills are being used;
- that each governor has a fair opportunity to contribute (and uses it);
- that the board receives the information it needs to meet its responsibilities; and
- that the meetings are conducted efficiently and reach clear conclusions.

AGBIS can also offer help and advice at reasonable cost, by conducting a more formal review process. A typical review is conducted over two days, by a team of two trained people: a member of the AGBIS board and either its general secretary or its training and membership secretary. It covers such matters as the duties and responsibilities of governors; board structures; committee cohesion and terms of reference; skills-set, nomination, recruitment and succession planning; new governor induction; sound financial management, controls and audit; how both to support and appropriately challenge the management; how to assess strategy; good internal communication; and how to make sure that all governors feel fully involved.

Specific training/review packages can be agreed with individual schools.

In all these areas, it is always a pleasure to try to help, endeavouring to make our much-admired schools even better and to support those who give their time and talent so generously. If in doubt, it is better to be pro-active – *ie* to ask sooner rather than later.

Chapter 20

How good are your meetings?

The first AGBIS e-Newsletter (December 2011) posed this question, and provided a checklist which we have reproduced below – with thanks to Carol Carty, AGBIS Communications Manager, and Nigel Noble, Training and Membership Secretary, who compiled it.

A lot of time is spent preparing for or attending meetings of the governing body (and its committees). Is this time well spent? Try answering the questions below and come to a view on the room for improvement in your governing body.

- Is your meetings programme published well in advance – *eg* by March for the following academic year?
- How involved is your Head in the preparation of the meeting agenda?
- Does the agenda make clear where governors are required to receive recommendations and make decisions; where they are to ratify decisions made under delegated powers, and where they are to note a report or information?
- Does the agenda provide a time plan for the meeting?
- Does your Chairman of governors receive a more detailed agenda with prompts to cover important items of business and potential areas of difficulty?
- Does the clerk sit next to the Chairman and help him or her to run the meeting?
- Do you receive your briefing pack at least seven days before the meeting? Do you have the option of receiving the pack in paper or digital format?
- Is the briefing pack limited to the agenda, Head's report, strategic plan update, committee minutes and reports for the governing body?
- Are longer papers and reports covered by an executive summary that covers the subject, the options, the recommended option and the action required of governors?

- Do you have a governors' portal on your network or website, where other documents (e.g. papers considered by committees) can be made available to governors?
- Do you have standard rule that governors are expected to have read the documents in the briefing pack and, if required, to have conducted further research via the governors' portal, and gone on to prepare questions and comments?
- Is the meeting room properly prepared - *eg* water, refreshments and note paper?
- Do those presenting committee minutes and reports briefly provide any additional information subsequent to the meeting, and then invite discussion and questions on the recommendations?
- Does the Chairman keep good control of the meeting? Do governors speak through the Chairman and only with his or her permission? Is there a culture of respect and brevity around the meeting table?
- Does the Chairman encourage views from all governors and bring them into the debate?
- Does your Chairman impose limits on the debate and ensure that the governing body does not replicate the work of a committee or all allow its work to be unpicked?
- In closing the agenda item, does your Chairman summarise the key issues and seek agreement or a formal resolution and vote?
- In approving recommendations or making decisions on other matters, are they considered in the context of your strategic plan objectives?
- Many decisions made by governors require time and considerable management action to implement. Does your governing body maintain an Action List that allows governors to monitor this implementation process?
- Are papers tabled at the meeting and are governors required to make decisions based only on a cursory review of their contents?
- Does the meeting end with a quick review of the meeting and its effectiveness?
- Are the resulting minutes clear and concise, and do they provide clear indications of why decisions were made?
- And finally, was there an appropriate balance between operational and strategic issues?

Conclusion and overview

Stuart Westley

Right at the start of this book my co-editor observed that governance is now a far more complex and demanding process than in days gone by. If you read the introduction and are now reading this conclusion, it is likely that you will have also digested the chapters in between, which demonstrated why this is so.

In the end, however, governance may occasionally be stressful and time-consuming, but should mostly be interesting and pleasurable. It is more likely to be the latter, if you keep four key principles in mind.

First, *the roles of governance and management are complementary but different*, and neither side should confuse them. *Guidelines for Governors* has been explicit on this principle for some 25 years and remains so. Governors are there to oversee; to praise or from time to time constructively to criticise; occasionally to take difficult decisions and to be unpopular, but *not* to micro-manage. It is worth reflecting on the sheer impracticality of even contemplating the relentless daily stream of issues that arise in our schools being addressed by a committee that meets once each term. Similarly we should remind ourselves that individual governors have no authority; it is the board collectively that has the authority and the responsibility. The board guards the ethos and the long-term interests of the school; its members oversee good practice, consistent with legal and charity requirements. They should not be control freaks. The Head and bursar and their teams exist to carry out the policy agreed by the governors; to run the school day-to-day and to report to the board truthfully, self-critically and effectively.

Secondly, *governors must ensure that they do nothing that unreasonably undermines those in management*. They must be very clear about who is in daily charge of the school: in almost all cases this is the Head. In a school in which the Head combines the roles of educational *and* financial supremo as CEO, it is particularly important that there is a clear line of reporting and accountability.

Conversely, governors must seek to avoid any situation in which those who are line-managed by the Head and bursar can use governors as a back door to avoid going through the proper channels. Sharper-eyed readers will have noted more than one situation in this book describing a situation in which a governor deals directly with another figure in the senior management. In an increasingly complex and specialist world, it can be a great advantage to tap fully into the expertise of members of the board in certain areas, but it is crucially important that those at the top of the management are fully aware of contacts between governors and other members of the senior management team; of contacts between governors and non-SMT staff, and the results of such contact.

Thirdly; *governors have a particular responsibility to set the strategy* – and by implication to ensure that the school does indeed *have* a strategy that is kept under regular review. This may seem obvious, but a surprising number of schools neglect it: for each one in which the board needs to restrain an over-enthusiastic and precipitate Head, there is likely to be another where the Head manages to keep the board satisfied by providing it only with management information rather than the broad ideas and supporting data that it really needs. Which is better use of a busy board's time: considering how it might respond to a major change in the provision of independent education in its locality, or poring match-by-match over the results of the Junior Colts 4th XV?

Heads and bursars should reflect carefully on what they report to governors. Governors need to be presented with a fair, balanced account of the important aspects of the life of the school – detailed, but not too detailed – and particularly of those aspects that relate to strategy. Undue emphasis on the detail and over-enthusiastic prose inevitably raise questions about judgement and the ability of the management to perceive the larger picture. In difficult economic times it is ever more important to be strategically proactive, even speculative, than to be rushed later into reacting to events that have already taken place.

Finally, *the key people in a good school should be well supported by good governors*. It is often said that a Head's job is a lonely one – and so, increasingly, is a bursar's. Their roles are unlikely to become any easier in the years ahead, either in terms of workload or the economic climate in which they find themselves working. They spend much of their day not just organising resources; arranging things; motivating and occasionally disciplining a wide variety of people, but also in providing pastoral care, both for adults and pupils. As the penultimate section of chapter 8 implied, someone needs to care for the carers – a thought well worth bearing in mind as you turn to the more light-hearted piece that follows.

Afterword

The bursar's wicked way with governors

David Goucher

Schools and businesses are overseen in a number of differing respects. One of the bigger differences lies in the numerical balance of executives and non-executives at board meetings. In business the two categories of directors may well be represented in more or less equal numbers, whereas in many schools the only executive figures present are the Head and the bursar, meeting with a board of 20 governors.

Much has already been written in this book about relationships between governors and Heads, but rather less about governors and bursars. In the early 1990s David Goucher, then bursar of Bryanston, wrote six articles for HMC's magazine Conference & Common Room, *published by John Catt Educational Ltd. In them he gave a tongue-in-cheek picture of a bursar's dealings with the various constituencies that constitute a school community.*

The articles had a common title: 'The bursar's wicked way with...'. An edited version of the various bursarial ploys for dealing with Heads; common room members; parents; pupils and other bursars appeared in volume 7 of this series.

We are very grateful to David Goucher for permission to reproduce this one in full. Most of the tactical considerations offered to bursars could apply equally well to – albeit that the examples of topics under discussion might be different...

The really well organised bursar will not only have the common room eating out of his hand and the Head generously topping up his sherry glass during their weekly *tête-a-têtes* but will also, equally adeptly, be working his wicked way with the school's governing body. It is not enough to acknowledge that those who hire may also fire, and that some governors proudly sport a collection of bursars' scalps: a pro-active strategy is needed to avoid the inevitable extra work falling upon the bursar in endless pursuit of their bright ideas and also to nullify the natural pre-disposition of governors for asking awkward questions. On the face of it, that might seem to be obstructing their very *raison d'être* and so be an impossible task. Not so. Those who seek assiduously to master *The art of coarse bursarship* have available a tantalising array of ploys and techniques with which to charm, disarm, and seduce even the most tenacious and incisive Board of governors.

The handbook of military strategy requires that you first of all know your enemy. So, too, with the bursar's approach towards the governors notwithstanding that, in this case, the 'enemy' is excessively friendly. The very nature of all governors is that of warm heartedness and generosity of spirit, not least towards the bursar they have themselves judiciously appointed and in whom they wish to see the vindication of their wise selection. Herein lies the key to understanding. Since most governors will already have achieved their primary life goals – high career progression, professional and public recognition, a house in the country, a time-share in the Algarve or wherever – they have all come to that point in life when they wish to 'put something back'. What other motive could possibly persuade them to accept responsibilities that, with no pecuniary reward, oblige them to sacrifice so many precious evenings and weekends, sometimes travelling hundreds of miles in foul weather, to sit through hours of council and sub-committee meetings, to endure Speech Days and Founders' Days and to put up with any amount of parental and OB obloquy accusing them of presiding over falling standards? An appreciation of such admirable altruism is the basis for a strategy that will secure a long, happy and untroubled relationship with the governors.

The astute bursar, aware that – above all – the governors want to feel good about what they are doing, will ensure that they are thoroughly and meticulously briefed on all the achievements and successes of 'Their School'. The Head can always be relied upon to highlight the school's spectacular academic, sporting and extracurricular triumphs but the governors will gain much vicarious satisfaction from hearing that the newly-built school laundry has exceeded all expectations in cost-effectiveness; that a 15 per cent discount has been skilfully negotiated on the window-cleaning contract, or even that the school has recently hosted the annual regional bursars' conference, omitting to mention, of course, that it was Buggin's turn. Modesty is quite out of place: it is a cardinal bursarial duty to bring to the notice of the governing body how well the school (and the bursar), is doing, and how ably it is being managed (by the bursar). By the same token, while giving the governors credit for all things bright and beautiful, bad news should be carefully sifted out.

And if, by some mischance, something has not gone terribly well and must be reported: say the flooding of the new all-weather pitch, it is vital that no blame should attach to the board even if the construction company was highly recommended by several members. Equally, you have to make absolutely sure that no blame attaches to the bursar either. Put it down to freak storms; an unforeseen rise in the water table; or blame it on the recession, currently a convenient excuse for all manner of ills. You will naturally wish to brief the Chairman beforehand and let him break the bad news; sudden bombshells from the bursar at council meetings are not well received.

The establishment of the right sort of employer/employee relationship stems from a careful individual appreciation of each governor and their areas of special interest. It is quite likely that one will be paranoiac about the arithmetical accuracy of the financial accounts and will inevitably spot an error: make sure that you find it first. Another, perhaps Brigadier Pedant OBE, will search your papers for a split infinitive or other grammatical goofs (the Army Staff College has much to answer for; or should that read 'For much has the Army Staff College to answer'?) The state of the drains and the fabric of the buildings might well be a constant source of anxiety to the clerical governor who will need to be plied with regular reassuring survey reports.

Old Boy governors should be treated with particular sensitivity but they can usually be won over by introducing frequent whiffs of nostalgia into your social conversation. Potentially the most irritating (to the bursar) will be the governor who is preoccupied with the welfare of the teaching staff, usually referring to them as 'the front line troops'. Avoiding at all costs another fundamental review of the teaching salary scale: the ploy here is to take every opportunity of drawing attention to the wide range of fringe benefits enjoyed by teachers – such as their direct and uncontrolled access to the photocopier; the discount on referees' whistles at the school shop; loan of the school's National Trust membership card or the free recreational use of the swimming pool when it is not hired out to other organisations.

Your strategy here should be to avoid a situation in which all the governors feel free to conduct an interrogation on any topic; try to persuade your Chairman to assign specific areas of interest to each governor, preferably well away from their normal area of expertise. Then, out of courtesy to each other, they will refrain from asking potentially awkward questions relating to a colleague's bailiwick. The perfect balance is achieved when each governor believes that he or she is making a worthwhile and specific contribution but does not get so closely involved that the bursar has to cancel a game of golf to show governors round the school's boiler houses.

It might be tempting to think, because the bursar is usually the clerk to the governing body and so compiles the briefing papers for meetings, that it might be relatively easy to manipulate the Board to the 'right' conclusions. Be very careful. Never underestimate your governors. How-ever much they might wish to go with the school, always bear in mind that they would not have achieved a certain pre-eminence in their professions and in public life if they were not reasonably astute. You may find it easy to work your wicked way with the common room but it must be remembered that most governors have been recruited from real life. It is fascinating and perhaps disturbing how frequently bursars contrast the way in which schools are run with real life.

By all means flatter your governors with carefully prepared papers and with concise and helpful summaries of the issues to be addressed, but do not expect them to be read, nor to be rubber stamped; governors do not take kindly to being taken for granted. The technique here, employing

US politico-military jargon, is to offer a choice of 'yes-able propositions'. If the ground has been properly prepared, your most yes-able proposition will be adopted. Wherever possible, you should not burden the governors with problems or difficult decisions without offering possible solutions; ideally, you should keep problems well away from the governors altogether for, if tempted to intervene, they might make the wrong decision – wrong in so far as it might disturb the bursar's equanimity. On the same tack, Head and bursar confrontations in front of the governors must never be allowed; if you cannot present a united front you will need to find either a new Head or a new job. Where governors are left to resolve such disputes, the track record heavily favours keeping the Head in post.

After the governors have dispersed, keep the minutes of the meeting as short as possible, thereby minimising your workload and the potential for error. A good way of avoiding subsequent amendments is not to invite them by attributing remarks to individual governors; they are bound to want the record changed to what they thought they said. All that is needed is a succinct statement of the issue, a brief resume of the discussion and a simple record of the decision. An 'action' column in the right-hand margin is essential for follow-up work, placing as much action as possible with the bursar, thereby attracting simultaneously both admiration for your sheer capacity and sympathy from those who have added to your burdens.

One final ploy: when arranging meetings, do make sure that there is a constant supply of hot coffee, fruit juice and chocolate biscuits – preferably those thickly coated chocolate biscuits that come individually wrapped. That will really make the governors feel good.

On the other hand, you might prefer to follow the advice given to me by a chairman of the finance and general purposes committee when I asked how a bursar might most successfully endear himself to the governing body. Wearing several scalps (and a few obvious scars), he advised that a bursar need only succeed in meeting three responsibilities: 1. Get the numbers right; 2. Get the numbers right; 3. Get the numbers right. *Gaudeamus igitur.*

For further reading

A list of chapters in other titles in this series

The bursar and the bursarial team — Annika Hedrich-Wiggans

An introductory guide to child protection — Nigel Richardson

Policy statements and the rolling review — Mike Vacher

Strategic planning; finance and budgeting issues; presenting accounts — Yvonne Thomas

Buildings and maintenance — Richard Metcalfe

Large-scale strategic planning and project management — Alison Shakespeare

Clerk to the governors — Roy Blackwell

People: legal issues that bursars may encounter — Bryan Login

'Non-people' legal issues that bursars may encounter — Alison Martin

Recruiting a bursar — Andy Dorgan

The bursar in a boarding school — Mark Taylor

Schools as charities: what difference does charitable status make? — Ray Maher

Managing ICT and its spending — Bruno Delacave

Lord High Everything Else — John Pratten

Getting the nost out of the ISBA — Paul Motte

Conclusion and overview — Jonathan Cook

Afterword: extracts from *The bursar's wicked way* — David Goucher

For further details, please see
http://johncattbookshop.com/Leading_Schools_in_the_21st_Century-list.aspx